WITH NO REMORSE

With No Remorse

Murder and Mayhem in our Schools—A Biblical Response

Tom Allen

HORIZON BOOKS
A division of Christian Publications, Inc.
Camp Hill, Pennsylvania

HORIZON BOOKS
A division of Christian Publications, Inc.
3825 Hartzdale Drive, Camp Hill, PA 17011
www.cpi-horizon.com

With No Remorse
ISBN: 0-88965-183-3

Printed in the United States of America

99 00 01 02 03 5 4 3 2 1

This book is dedicated to

Arliss:

A lovely wife,
an excellent mother
and gifted teacher,
making a difference in the lives
of junior high students

Contents

Part 2
Natural Born Causes

Part 3
The Supernatural Cure

Foreword

I have known Tom Allen a long time—and his father, Bill, before him. Tom's dad was a pastor, but certainly not a typical one. He was engaged in his community more than most—and he was fearless. He was particularly adept at engaging men—powerful men before whom others often hesitated. But not Bill Allen.

Tom has some of his dad's audacity. It served him well in his recent book, *A Closer Look at Dr. Laura*, in which he carefully analyzes the philosophy and theology of Dr. Laura Schlessinger.

In *With No Remorse*, his best work yet, he gets to underlying issues about violence in our schools. He answers the "why" question clearly and courageously.

Tom Allen has engaged the culture of violence and death with a touch of his father's audacity. The result is a definitive book on guns and violence, a popular analysis that makes profound sense. I enthusiastically commend it to you.

K. Neill Foster

President/Publisher, Christian Publications, Inc.

Acknowledgments

I want to express my gratitude to Dr. K. Neill Foster and his excellent staff at Christian Publications. We've been working together for twenty-two years, and I have always appreciated their respect for me as a writer. I am indebted to them for their fine job of editing and publishing.

This project has been bathed in prayer, and I want to thank each and every one who has interceded for this important book. I humbly acknowledge my complete dependence on God for this gift of writing.

As always, a special thanks to my wife, Arliss, and daughters, Andrea and Amanda, for their patience, love and support.

Introduction

The Doomsday Dozen

October 27, 1999. "Good evening. We now have a clearer picture of the group responsible for the worst mass murder in the history of the United States. One thousand twenty-three students and staff were killed Monday morning at Grand High School in Grand Lakes, Minnesota. The entire building was leveled in a firestorm of explosions; there were no survivors. We are in possession of a detailed diary which outlines the methodical plotting of this monstrous act—the work of 'The Doomsday Dozen.'

"Their first planning meeting was the day after the shootings in Littleton, Colorado—April 20, 1999. The entire country was still trying to grasp the enormity of the tragedy at Columbine High School: fifteen dead; twenty-three wounded; adolescent executioners in black trench coats; an overwhelming arsenal. But the task of Eric Harris and Dylan Klebold was not finished. In fact, these twelve terrorists were quite certain they could do a better job. That was the subject of their initial scheming.

"Though these high school juniors and seniors in rural Minnesota called themselves 'The Doomsday Dozen,' no one else knew about this name. They had learned the lessons of Littleton: no web site, no sign that they were a clique at school. They only wore their distinctive clothing—brown leather bomber jackets—during their secret meetings. And another distinguishing characteristic: this group included two females.

"Consumed with alienation and anger like the murderers who had gone before them, they were futureless. The Doomsday Dozen had chosen the day of their deaths. They would take hundreds with them—and on a very special day. In the Harris/Klebold tradition, they used a date from the life of Adolph Hitler: October 25, the day in 1956 when Hitler's remains had been positively identified and he was officially declared dead. It only seemed fitting that Doomsday should celebrate this madman's demise. Two days ago, it happened at 10 a.m. on October 25, 1999.

"With six months of careful planning, The Doomsday Dozen built and bought sophisticated and compact explosive devices. Through incredibly advanced computer technology, all of the bombs were tied into one remote detonating device. At exactly 10 a.m., these twelve 'apostles from hell' stood on the hillside above the school and, with the push of a button, more than 1,000 people were instantly destroyed. Then, according to the diary, Jonas Springfield, their leader, executed the other eleven members with single shots to their heads and then turned the gun on himself. The bodies were found just as he had written.

"The nation is mourning the unthinkable. Who could have imagined in their darkest nightmare that something much worse than the massacre in Littleton, Colorado would occur in the same year? Stunned politicians, pastors, psychologists and educators are asking the now familiar question with an even greater incertitude: why?"

My opening story, though fictional, is no longer untenable. By the time this book is in print, North America may already be dealing with another tragic school shooting. Many students and educators have had this nagging question lingering in the back of their minds: "Who has been planning what over the summer months?"

Is there another terrorist tag team like Eric Harris and Dylan Klebold plotting someone else's destruction in a dimly lit basement or garage somewhere in suburbia? Who else is ready to explode because of anger, alienation or rejection? Will the body count grow larger as teens callously compete for their place in history?

During my very first week of writing this book, the rage floated a bit too close to my own shoreline. My wife, a teacher at a local junior high school, received a letter from her principal which started out like this:

> We have had two incidents occur at school this past week that you need to be aware of. Both incidents involved students who admitted to writing so-called "hit lists" in the past. One was written sometime in January, and the other was written at the end of March. . . .

Along with three other teachers, my wife was on one of those lists! Even though the school has dealt appropriately with each boy involved, we have had some anxious moments. Everything we had been watching on TV and listening to on the radio suddenly became more real and threatening. The violence "out there in another state" was suddenly much closer to home.

Having experienced our fifth major school shooting incident in three years, our nation is just now waking up to the fact that this kind of madness could truly happen anywhere. The first few occurrences produced predictable answers:

"It was a rural area."

"He was emotionally troubled."

"They came from broken homes."

But as we will see, the gunmen at Columbine High School did not fit into any of those categories. Furthermore, those explanations just don't fit these crimes. Something else is going on here.

We are right to cast a suspicious glance in several directions: violent video games, absent and careless parents, unrestrained savagery on television and in movies, music filled with death and destruction, the ubiquitous Internet with its World Wide Web of iniquity. Certainly these things must have something to do with the unprecedented carnage we are witnessing around the nation. I will have much more to say about each of these powerful forms of influence in Part 2.

But after all of this has been analyzed to death, there is still a nagging, haunting feeling that we have not really gotten to the bottom of this.

There is something going on here that defies all of the previously held theories on what motivates murder. Psychologists and social workers have been humbled in the recognition that their stock answers just don't fit these atrocities. Kids killing kids and teachers is a category of crime that takes the subject to a whole new level.

Following the catastrophe in Colorado, *Newsweek* and *U.S. News & World Report* magazines had a single word in huge letters on their covers: WHY? *Time* referred to the murderous teens as "The Monsters Next Door," and asked, "What made them do it?" Nancy Gibbs offered this lament: "The hardest thing about the search for an explanation was the growing fear there might not be one."[1]

This book takes up the challenge of answering the terrifying "WHY?" question. I believe there is an explanation for these tragic, violent eruptions among our teenagers. And though I am the first to agree with those who say that ultimately these mass murders result from a confluence of factors, there is one key to it all that has been ignored, dismissed or simply misunderstood.

There are droves of analysts who have made noble attempts to piece together partial interpretations of these horrific events. However, they are not too dogmatic in their assertions.

But I contend that they are missing the central reason behind these confounding crimes.

So, read carefully with an open mind. There is an answer. There is hope.

Part 1

Natural Born Killers

"In one scene of Oliver Stone's film Natural Born Killers *the hero drowns his girlfriend's father in a fish tank and kills her mother by tying her down on the bed, pouring gasoline on her and burning her alive. Meanwhile, a raucous, laugh-filled sound track tells the audience to regard this slaughter as the funniest thing in the world."* [1]

—Lynne Cheney, Fellow,
American Enterprise Institute

I am very proud to say that I have not seen this morbid movie. From the reviews that I've read, it is the sordid tale of a deadly duo, Mickey and Mallory Knox (played by Woody Harrelson and Juliette Lewis). Plagued with horrifying nightmares and memories of their troubled childhoods, the Knoxes embark on a trail of merciless, ultra-violent killings. This couple without a conscience is captivated by delusions of grandeur and warped concepts of reality.

The director of *Natural Born Killers*, Oliver Stone, was quoted as saying this about audience reaction to his film: "The most pacifistic person in the world came out of that movie wanting to kill somebody." [2]

Evidently, Mr. Stone would consider the film a great success for that reason.

But setting aside my sense of disgust about his gratuitous ode to violence, there is something about that title that rings true. *Natural born killers*—let that sink in for a moment. The movie is about people whose very nature seemed to drive them to profane, murderous acts. Born to brutalize. Computerized for carnage.

In Part 1, I want to introduce you to several individuals who fit this profile. They are indeed "natural born killers." But the big surprise will be this: many of them will seem just like you and me. And therein lies the catch. These murderers *are* very much like us. The startling truth behind that similarity will be revealed in Part 2.

Chapter 1

The New Profile of a Mass Murderer

"Most rampagers tend to save the last bullet for themselves. Those that don't are usually declared legally insane."

—From the web page *www.mayhem.net*

Research for a book like this takes one to strange web sites. Case in point: *www.mayhem.net*. This is where you are taken when you look up things like "serial killers" and "mass murderers" with a search engine. I had no idea that someone had taken the time to catalog every gory detail of our nation's prolific homicidal history. The understatement of the year is to call this merely a "frightening" web site.

Richard Speck, John Wayne Gacy, Ted Bundy—they are all there, with graphic details of their savagery, including body counts. As you move the cursor to other categories, you hear the sound of a gunshot—a touch of realism. The bloodshed represented on those pages is chilling to contemplate. It is difficult to think about the thousands of families whose innocent sons or daughters, parents or grandparents were alive and well one day and dead the next. It is impossible to calculate the human agony embodied in those pages.

The authorities on mayhem and massacres have divided things into neat categories for us. Here are the basic profiles:

Serial Killers

- Sexually dysfunctional, white, male
- Age: late twenties to late thirties
- Low self-esteem
- Crimes are usually sexual in nature

Mass Murderers

- Male, white, conservative
- Age: late twenties to late thirties
- Come from relatively stable, lower middle-class backgrounds
- See ambitions thwarted and blame others for keeping them down[1]

Ranking Mass Murderers

The web site ominously informs us that "because of its ever-increasing size, the Mass Murderer Hit List has been broken into three sections according to number of hits."[2]

The categories are then listed as:

- Eight or more hits
- Between five & eight hits
- Less than five hits

The top-ranked mass murderers of our time are Timothy J. McVeigh and his cohort Terry Nichols. Their rage was reportedly fueled by the FBI's fiery attack on a religious cult in Waco, Texas. So on April 19, 1995, they blew up the Alfred P. Murrah building in Oklahoma City. A total of 168 people did not return home that day.

In third place is Andrew Kehoe. On May 18, 1927, he blew up a school in Bath, Michigan. Of the forty-five people killed, thirty-seven were small children.

David Burke is the fifth most destructive mass murderer. Pacific Southwest Airlines fired Mr. Burke—and on December 7, 1987, he got revenge. He followed his ex-boss on to a plane and shot him midway through the flight. The plane crashed, killing all forty-three people on board.[3]

Number Fifteen

Down the list in the number fifteen ranking is a relatively new pair of killers: Eric Harris and Dylan Klebold. They executed twelve students and one teacher before committing suicide inside the school library at Columbine High School in Littleton, Colorado. But here's the most shocking aspect of all: the numbers that follow their names.

Eric Harris, eighteen.
Dylan Klebold, seventeen.

We are forced to look twice—and then a third time—at those ages. This simply does not fit the "mass murderer" profile in anyone's FBI manual. There must be some mistake. The other killers in this category had many more years to accumulate the bitterness and hatred that precipitated such widespread slaughter. But teenagers? Someone please check those birth certificates! In a world where strange things happen all the time, this would seem to win the award for most bizarre.

The number of teen killers has been steadily on the rise in the past three years. Even a jaded culture like ours has been shaken out of its apathetic slumber in response to this adolescent fury. Most of us remember a very different society in the not-too-distant past.

When I was in junior high and high school (1966-1972), rage was expressed quite differently. If someone was jealous of or mad at one of the "jocks," he would simply challenge him to a fistfight in the woods. I watched a few of those brawls. They didn't last long, but when it was over, it was over. Rarely did the same two guys fight again. The boys had "gotten it out of their systems." The goal was to humiliate and dominate—not annihilate. The idea of killing someone you didn't like was unthinkable.

An Early Addiction to Violence

What has so dramatically changed our culture in the last few decades? How is it that our young people have become addicted to violence in its most lethal form? What has driven down the age limit for those involved in mass murder and mayhem? Bob Herbert ruminates on this matter in the *New York Times*:

> Welcome to America, a land where the killing is easy. We are so familiar with this kind of story that news organizations across the country moved effortlessly to cover it. We've all seen it before. . . . We make it exciting. We celebrate it, romanticize it, eroticize it and mass-market the weapons that bring murder within easy reach of one and all. We are addicted to violence. It sustains and entertains us. . . . We'll move on until the next time, when another dozen or so kids are killed, or something worse happens. Then we'll throw up our hands again and ask what went wrong. It's like that with an addiction. Nothing happens until you admit you have a problem.[4]

Indeed we do have a problem. And it is unlike anything we have ever seen before in North America. With no remorse, young people are arming themselves to the teeth and blowing away their peers and professors. It is doubtless the worst possible nightmare for the evolutionist who fancied that the human race should have progressed much further along the path to peaceful coexistence. The utopian dreams of our humanist philosophers have been shattered into tiny pieces.

We are stuck with this new profile of a mass murderer. It has, in fact, signaled an acceleration in the process of "devolution." Webster's defines devolution as "retrograde evolution . . . degeneration." Rather than taking steps in a positive direction, our race seems hell-bent on a journey into the vortex of unprecedented violence and destruction. We are into some dangerous quicksand that threatens to pull us even deeper into evil. We may not be far from the day when every American will be held hostage to fear and torment.

Perhaps none of this murder and mayhem has touched you or me personally just yet. But now many of us are convinced that it could. Just acknowledging this fact has made us think twice about saying a simple good-bye to our kids as they leave for school in the morning. We know that some students in Pearl, Mississippi; Paducah, Kentucky; Jonesboro, Arkansas; Eugene, Oregon; and Littleton, Colorado never made it home after school one day.

Dr. James Garbarino has been catapulted into the media spotlight by an eerie coincidence of timing. His book *Lost Boys* was released the same week as the massacre in Littleton, Colorado. He addressed a group of educators at the Landmark Center in St. Paul, Minnesota, on May 11. I attended the lecture, and he made some excellent points.

In his introduction he openly admitted that the typical white person in America has had a naive arrogance about youth violence: "You're safe if you're white and middle or upper class—that's an inner-city dilemma." But he points out that the shootings that have occurred these past few years have dramatically changed all of this. Our immunity has evaporated. Vulnerability has replaced it.

I taught a class on creative writing in a local middle school one week after the tragedy at Columbine High School. As I walked in the building, it occurred to me that something wicked could be brewing in this building too. The kids looked utterly "normal"—just like Eric Harris and Dylan Klebold did in their senior pictures published in *Time*. But who might be holding a grudge in this school? Who might have easy access to guns? Who was about to explode?

Why did I have such gruesome thoughts swirling in my head? Because it's a new world. We have a novel problem that is unlike any we have faced before. And we have a new profile for mass murderers.

In the next chapter, we will consider the sad history of teens who have committed mass murders. Then, in chapters 3 through 7, we will take a look at the five major school shootings in the U.S. between October 1997 and April 1999.

Chapter 2

Monday, Monday

"I just don't like Mondays. . . . I did this because it's a way to cheer up the day." [1]

—Brenda Spencer

Today she is serving the twentieth year of a twenty-five-years-to-life sentence. She will be eligible for a parole hearing in 2001. She is incarcerated for killing the principal and a custodian at the Cleveland Elementary School in the San Carlos neighborhood of San Diego, California. Eight children and one police officer were also wounded in the attack.

Her name is Brenda Spencer. She was sixteen at the time of her killing spree. When asked why she was firing her .22-caliber rifle at the school yard across the street, her explanation was incredibly casual comment quoted above: "I just don't like Mondays. . . . I did this because it's a way to cheer up the day." She spoke with reporters by telephone as she held off the

San Diego police for six hours that day in February, 1979. When they asked her whom she was trying to kill, Ms. Spencer said rather matter-of-factly, "No one in particular. I kind of like the red and blue jackets."

After several hours of futile attempts to get Brenda to surrender, she finally decided it was time to end what she had called "fun." She walked calmly out of the house and put her gun down, then went back inside and waited for the police to arrest her. An eight-year-old asked, "Why did she do it?" *Time* magazine concluded sadly, "Unfortunately, no one in authority could answer that question."[2]

Brenda Spencer was cold. Calculated. She had no remorse.

Staggering Numbers

In his book, *Lost Boys,* Dr. James Garbarino offers this staggering numerical summary:

> The FBI reports that there are about twenty-three thousand homicides each year in the United States. In about 10 percent of these cases, the perpetrator is under eighteen years of age. If we extend the age cutoff to include youth up to the age of twenty-one, the figure is about 25 percent.[3]

Pause for a moment and let this sink in:

2,300 murders committed each year by those under eighteen

-or-

5,750 murders committed each year by those under twenty-one

To make matters even worse, Dr. Garbarino points out that these numbers are lower than they could be because of advances in medicine. An injury that would have been fatal just twenty years ago is today much less likely to result in death. He cites an example from Chicago. From the mid-1970s to the mid-1990s, the number of serious assaults (attacks that could lead to the death of the victim) increased a whopping 400 percent. During that same time period, however, the homicide rate remained essentially the same.

Here are some other shocking statistics:

- The average age of perpetrators of homicide decreased in the United States from thirty-three in 1965 to twenty-seven in 1993.
- While the overall homicide rate has been relatively constant over the last thirty years, the youth murder rate has risen.
- From the mid-1980s to the mid-1990s, the youth homicide rate increased 168 percent.
- The youth suicide rate has skyrocketed 400 percent since 1950.[4]

These numbers seem so shocking because so many of these brutal crimes do not make the national news. The media tends to become more infatuated with the tragedies that occur in suburbia. Inner-city homicides committed by young people are no longer front-page news—not even in the cities where they occur. But wherever young men and women are killing with no remorse, we must be alert to the message that is being sent.

Timeline of Terror

Consider some more examples of mass murder masterminded by young men and women:

- In 1951, Kenneth Skinner, seventeen, burned an apartment building in San Francisco. Eight people died. Although the building was on his paper route, he said he did not know any of the victims.
- Charles Starkweather was nineteen in 1958 when he led his girlfriend, Caril Fugate, fourteen, on a week-long killing spree. They shot, stabbed and strangled eleven people in Nebraska and Wyoming. Hours before his death in the electric chair, Starkweather was asked if he would donate his eyes for medical use. "H—, no," he said. "No one ever did anything for me. Why should I do anything for anyone else?"
- Charles Whitman was an expert marksman and a former Eagle Scout and Marine. In July 1966 he killed his wife and his mother. Then he took a footlocker full of ammunition, shotguns, rifles, Spam sandwiches and water to a twenty-seven-story clock tower at the University of

Texas in Austin, where he was a junior. From there, he shot forty-six people in ninety minutes. Sixteen were dead by the time the police killed him.

- "I just wanted to get myself a name." That is what motivated Robert Benjamin Smith, eighteen, to take seven female hostages in a beauty salon in Mesa, Arizona. He fatally shot five of them, including a three-year-old girl. Though sentenced to die, Smith won an appeal and remains in prison.
- "The pressure just got the best of me," said Anthony Barbaro, eighteen, just before he hanged himself in his prison cell. In 1974, he had entered his Olean, New York, high school during Christmas break and set several fires. A custodian who was investigating was gunned down by Barbaro. Then he went to a third floor window and shot at firefighters and passersby, killing two more people and wounding nine. An investigation of his home turned up handmade bombs and a diary detailing five months of planning the attack.[5]
- It was 2 p.m. on February 2, 1996. Barry Loukaitis, fourteen, opened fire with his .30-caliber rifle at Frontier Junior High in Moses Lake, Washington. One teacher and two students were killed, and one more wounded. He said he was influenced by the movie *Natural Born Killers* and Stephen King's book, *Rage*. He

is serving two life sentences at Clallam Bay Corrections Center.[6]

- February 19, 1997, Bethel, Alaska: Evan Ramsey, sixteen, paraded down the hallway of his high school toting a 12-gauge shotgun. He tracked down the principal and a student and shot them both to death. Ramsey later said he thought the shootings would be "cool." In December of 1998, he was sentenced to 210 years in prison.[7]
- A science teacher at West Parker Middle School was killed on April 24, 1998 in Edinboro, Pennsylvania, by fourteen-year-old Andrew Wurst. Another teacher and two other students were wounded as Wurst opened fire at a school dance.[8]
- Four days later—April 28, 1998—two boys, ages fourteen and seventeen, were shot to death on the Philadelphia Elementary School playground in Pomona, California. This was the result of a fight between two rival "party crews" which stage parties with music and disc jockeys. The murder was the work of a thirteen-year-old whose name was withheld by authorities.[9]
- A fourteen-year-old boy in Taber, Alberta, Canada, was charged on April 28, 1999 with first-degree murder and attempted murder in a shooting at the W.R. Myers High School that killed one student and seriously wounded another. He fired four shots from a .22-caliber rifle. It was the first fatal high school shooting

in Canada in twenty years. The father of the slain student, Rev. Dale Lang, said at a news conference, "May God have mercy on this broken society and all the hurting people in it."[10]

A Pattern Emerges

Caitlin Lovinger, who compiled most of the above list, said, "If the following examples fail to show a pattern, it may be because there is none."[11]

I totally disagree. There *is* a clear pattern here: Young men and women from relatively stable, middle-class homes just decided to start killing. They torched and tormented because they wanted to do it. With no sense of conscience for their victims or the maimed survivors, they willfully lit fires, thrust knives and pulled triggers. It doesn't sound pretty, but it's the horrible truth that unifies each of these barbaric acts.

The most troubling characteristic of natural born killers is that they can go on a murderous rampage and feel no remorse. They could not have cared less for those on the receiving end of their firebombs and gun barrels. They gave not a moment's thought to the parents, children and other relatives and friends who would suffer with the consequences of their random violence for a lifetime. It's about "cheering up the day," dealing with "pressure" or "making a name for myself." It is heartless.

Some of these stories date back to the relative innocence of the 1950s. This immediately challenges the notion that everything can be attributed to the Internet, lousy parenting, violent video games, TV, movies and other so-called "explanations" for mass-murdering teenagers. Though we will see that these aspects of our modern culture have accelerated the pace and intensity of lethal youth crime sprees, they can never be considered a "first cause." There can be only one first cause.

The Mamas and the Papas sang a doleful song in the 1960s called "Monday, Monday." It was about the jolt of reality that Monday often brings to those who partied a bit too much over the weekend. It started out, "Monday, Monday—can't trust that day."

Brenda Spencer shared this sentiment in a big way. She soothed her Monday blues by killing two adults and wounding eight children and a police officer. "I don't like Mondays. . . . I did this because it's a way to cheer up the day."

Those are the frightening words of a natural born killer.

Chapter 3

Gutsy and Daring

"Murder is not weak and slow-witted; murder is gutsy and daring." [1]

—Luke Woodham

It was a handwritten note given to a classmate on October 1, 1997, just moments before the loud noises began:

> I am not insane. I am angry. I killed because people like me are mistreated every day. I did this to show society: push us and we will push back. Murder is not weak and slow-witted, murder is gutsy and daring.[2]

Then the bullets started flying at about 8:10 a.m., as buses arrived at Pearl High School in Pearl, Mississippi. Luke Woodham, a sixteen-year-old sophomore, entered the large commons area just inside the front door of the school and walked up to his former girlfriend. She was the first to go down. She was shot point blank in the neck with a .30-.30 hunting rifle. Then three young men and four young women were apparently shot at random. Mark Wilkerson, a freshman, said, "He was shooting anybody he could find. He shot at me and hit the staircase."[3]

Students ran screaming into classrooms and dived for cover. One eyewitness said, "He was so cool and calm. I saw him shoot a kid, and he ejected the shell. He was walking along, thumbing fresh rounds into the side port of the rifle."[4]

As Luke Woodham tried to escape in his mother's vehicle, assistant principal Joel Myrick rammed his car into Woodham's. "I could see him sitting there, holding on to the steering wheel, his knuckles white, those glasses on him," Myrick recalls. "I kept asking him why, why, why. He said, 'Mr. Myrick, the world has wronged me.' "[5]

The police quickly arrested him and charged him with murder and aggravated assault. It appeared that he had killed two students, Christina Menefee, sixteen, and Lydia Kaye Dew, seventeen. Seven others were injured.

But there were two more bodies. One canine, one human. And they were not at the school.

In sickening detail, Luke Woodham described the torture and killing of the first victim: his own dog, Sparkle. Luke and an accomplice beat the pet savagely with clubs and then stuffed her in several plastic bags. They then doused the sack with lighter fluid and set it on fire before hurling it into a pond. The sight of the sinking bag, Woodham said, was "true beauty." In his own words:

> On Saturday of last week, I made my first kill. The victim was a loved one, my dear dog Sparkle. I will never forget the howl she made. It sounded almost human. We laughed and hit her more.[6]

The second victim was Mary Ann Woodham, fifty, a receptionist who had been divorced for five years. She usually drove her son Luke to school. But that day the corpse of Mrs. Woodham was discovered at her home about a mile from the school. Mary had been beaten with a baseball bat and repeatedly stabbed with a butcher knife. Authorities believe she was killed by her son about three hours before the shooting rampage at the school.

A Quiet Boy

Luke Woodham was known as a quiet boy. He was pudgy and shabbily dressed. But he never seemed to fight back when others called him names. Kids would knock books from his hands, and he took it without even swearing. Senior Stephanie Walker recalled, "He was picked on for as long as I can remember. Most people who aren't popular get picked on. I never heard him say a cuss word."[7]

The early explanation was that Woodham went on this killing spree because of his break-up with Christina Menefee. Christina was a bright, popular girl who excelled at math and biology and took part in Junior Naval ROTC. She had compassion for Luke because he was the frequent target of taunting and ridicule; she had a heart for the underdog. But they dated only briefly, and a year before she was killed, Christina broke off the relationship saying she wanted to see other boys. However, she was careful to let him down gently, and afterward there was no hint of trouble.

Even more puzzling was the murder of Luke's mother, Mary Ann Woodham. Mary was a concerned, perhaps even overprotective mom. Christina's parents recall that when Luke came to see their daughter, he would always bring along his mother—sort of a Southern custom. The boy suffered his mother's presence with only occasional hints of impatience. Most observers felt that Luke had a good relationship with his mother. His brutality was stunning beyond words.

Conspiracy Theories

Six friends of Luke Woodham's were arrested on October 7, 1997, on murder-conspiracy charges. This group of seven appears to have formed what they called "The Kroth"—a name perhaps culled from satanic literature. Though mostly good students, they were on the social fringes. They were involved in what seemed to be a feverish plot to rid themselves of their enemies and win the respect they felt they deserved.

According to police, the leader was Grant Boyette, an eighteen-year-old former student at Pearl High. A "self-proclaimed Satanist," Boyette admired Adolph Hitler and his tactics. He was impressed with the way *der Fuhrer* could influence people. Boyette considered himself to be the "father," with Luke Woodham as his pawn. Criminal investigator Greg Eklund alleged that "[Boyette] was the one that called the shots."[8]

The Kroth had developed a hit list, which included the mayor's son "for the shock value." This group had a penchant for black clothing and for the brooding nihilism of the nineteenth-century philosopher Friedrich Nietzsche. A page copied from Woodham's notebook contained a passage from Nietzsche's 1887 book, *The Gay Science*, with the philosopher's famous declaration: "God is dead. God remains dead. And we have killed him."[9]

Bill Hewett summarizes the consternation in the community as they became aware of the conspiracy:

> The notion of a dime-store fuhrer inspiring apostles of terror, along with prosecution allegations that the group practiced Satanism as a cult, has continued to send ripples of apprehension through the community and beyond. One neighboring school district canceled a pep rally out of fear that kids would be shot by members of the group who have yet to be arrested.[10]

Ricky Blailock had a fifteen-year-old daughter attending Pearl High School in 1997. He told the *Los*

Angeles Times, "It's the grip of evil is what it is. It's the grip of Satan. He's got a grip on this world like you wouldn't believe."[11]

Trials and Verdicts

In June 1998, Luke Woodham faced two trials: the first for the murder of his mother, the second for the murders and the maimings at Pearl High School. At his first trial on June 4, Woodham testified that he woke up on that October morning haunted by demons. These demons told him that he would be nothing unless he went to school and killed his targets. Woodham claimed that he tried to resist the voices, but he kept hearing his friend Boyette telling him "to do something." He said he could not remember the actual slaying of his mother. "I just closed my eyes and fought with myself because I didn't want to do any of it. When I opened my eyes, my mother was lying in her bed dead."[12]

On June 5, Woodham was found guilty of first-degree murder in the death of his mother. The jury in Philadelphia took less than four hours to convict him. Asked by the judge if he had anything to say, Mr. Woodham replied simply, "No, sir." Circuit Judge Samac Richardson had given the jurors the option of finding that Woodham wasn't responsible for his actions because he was mentally ill, as the defense had argued, but the judge refused to give them the choice of considering a manslaughter conviction instead of a murder charge.[13]

District Attorney John Kitchens produced two expert witnesses who testified that Luke Woodham was sane at the time of the killings. Kitchens expressed satisfaction that the jurors rejected the mental illness defense. "I commend them for seeing through this jail house defense that was concocted by Luke Woodham in this case."[14]

In his closing arguments, Assistant District Attorney Tim Jones described Woodham as "mean" and "hateful": "He's bloodthirsty. He wanted to kill her. Murder was on this boy's mind."[15]

At the second trial later in June, Woodham was carrying his Bible with him to court. He said that he found religion during his time in jail. He was pronounced guilty on two counts of murder and seven counts of aggravated assault. He was sentenced to two life terms plus seven twenty-year terms in prison. In an interview after his sentencing, Luke Woodham told an investigator for the Rankin County sheriff's office: "I know I did some bad things. This would not have happened if I had had God in my life."[16]

Romantic break-ups far outnumber the make-ups during the teen years. Although it is inexcusable, it is still a fact of life that pudgy, intellectual people are mocked and ridiculed every day in schools across the country. We are all subject to bad influences and bad people. Luke Woodham got As and Bs in school and was fortunate to have a mother who cared and wanted to be involved in his life. So why did he bludgeon his dog, butcher his mother and blast nine students with bullets from a hunting rifle?

The psychologists don't have a clue. It cannot be explained away with talk about his "toxic environment," his "abusive childhood" or any other victimization formula. Every indication is that Luke Woodham is another "natural born killer." Something about his very nature drove him to commit these heinous atrocities.

Meanwhile, the residents of Pearl, Mississippi, population 22,000, are left with the ramifications of his rampage. Mayor Jimmy Foster summed it up best:

> You know the old cliché—it happens to somebody else? It happened to us this time, and it was shocking. It cut through the heart of the community. What happened to us [that] morning was unthinkable. We won't ever get over it.[17]

Unfortunately, the "unthinkable" was about to happen again to "somebody else"—this time, during a prayer meeting.

Chapter 4

Death at a Prayer Meeting

"If Michael Carneal was a human time bomb, nobody seems to have heard him ticking. He had never been in trouble with the law, never displayed any violent behavior, never given anyone the least cause for fear." [1]

—Jonah Blank & Warren Cohen

Benjamin Strong was at the breakfast table that morning munching on Froot Loops and half-listening to his father. Rev. Strong was reading from the book of Proverbs, but Ben found it difficult to concentrate. The seventeen-year-old was pondering the words of a classmate. "Don't be at prayer circle on Monday. Something big is going to happen." Michael Carneal had told him that on the Wednesday before Thanksgiving.

Carneal was a bit of a misfit at Heath High School in West Paducah, Kentucky. He occasionally wore ill-fitting, loud-colored clothing. He had been disciplined twice: once for browsing the *Playboy* web site in the school library and another time for digging a sharp object into a classroom wall. But he could also discuss the Shakespeare play assigned to class (*Romeo and Juliet*) with allusions to other works by the bard.

Ben Strong was a senior. Michael Carneal was a freshman. They were in distinctly different social classes with Ben's father being a pastor and Michael's dad being a prominent lawyer. They were friends, however, and both played in the brass section of the band. "He just interested me," Strong told *Time*. "He seemed to be real."[2]

This is what made Benjamin Strong take the statement very seriously. He imagined everything from water guns to real guns. At the worst, he would just wave a gun around, right? Perhaps Michael was just being sarcastic when he issued the warning. *Don't be at prayer circle on Monday. Something big is going to happen.* But Strong could not stay away from the prayer meeting—he was *leading* it!

So before school on December 1, 1997, Ben Strong was leading that prayer group in the entrance hall when his worst nightmare came true. Ben saw Carneal enter the lobby, and in his closing prayer, he asked God for strength to last through the day. As the "Amen" was uttered, the thirty-five members of the prayer circle squeezed hands. Then something else was squeezed—a trigger.

Three loud pops. A pause. Then seven shots came out in perfect rhythm before another pause intervened. Anyone who knew anything about weapons would immediately recognize this as semiautomatic gunfire. Ben looked right at Michael and forcefully said, "Put down the gun!" But Carneal continued to fire from the 11-round clip. Strong yelled again as the other students ran for cover. "What are you doing?" Ben pleaded. "Don't shoot. Just put the gun down."

When Michael Carneal paused that second time, Strong took advantage of the situation and pounced on his friend, pinning him against the wall. The gun fell to their feet. As he gripped Carneal's hands, he could feel the trembling. An earplug fell from the shooter's ear. Finally Michael made eye contact with his friend and said in a cracking voice, "Kill me, please. I can't believe I did that."[3]

The principal of Heath High School, Bill Bond, jumped from his desk and ran to the lobby when he heard the gunshots. Bodies and blood were all over the floor. Crying and moaning. Then he spotted the Ruger .22 on the floor and the two students face-to-face. Bond kicked the gun away.

Three students were dead: Nicole Hadley, fourteen; Kayce Steger, fifteen; Jessica James, seventeen. Five others were injured; one was paralyzed from the waist down.

Thanksgiving Weekend

It could have been worse—much worse. McCracken County Sheriff Frank Augustus discovered an arsenal Carneal had amassed over the holiday weekend. On Thanksgiving he stole two shotguns, two semiautomatic rifles, a pistol and 700 rounds of ammunition—all from a neighbor's garage. He hauled the cache home with his bicycle and sneaked it into his bedroom through a window. He later told psychiatrists, "I was feeling proud, strong, good, and more respected. I had accomplished something. I'm not the kind of kid who accomplishes anything. This is the only adventure I've ever had."[4]

The next day he stole two more shotguns from his parents' bedroom. Then on Saturday he took "the best" guns to a friend's house where they admired them together and shot targets with a pistol. On Sunday, after church and homework, the arsenal was wrapped in a blanket. He would take the guns to school to show them off. In his own words, he expected that "[e]veryone would be calling me and they would come over to my house or I would go to their house. I would be popular."[5]

Monday, December 1, finally came. He put his bundle of weapons into the trunk of his sister's Mazda. The Ruger .22 pistol was in his backpack. When he arrived at school, he found his friends hanging out in the lobby and immediately announced what was in the blanket. He waited for their adulation. But no one was particularly impressed. In that part of Kentucky, firearms are a part of everyday life.

Disgusted by being ignored, he pulled the Ruger out of his backpack. Once again no one reacted. At 7:40 a.m., with three dead and five wounded on the blood-coated floor, Michael Carneal finally got noticed.

Personal and Family Matters

According to the evaluations, Michael never felt close to his father. His older sister, Kelly, seemed to get the lion's share of the family's attention. She was very popular. In fact, Kelly was the school valedictorian six months after the multiple murders by her brother. "He tries to be as good as me," she told psychiatrists, "and he can never size up."[6]

Michael compensated for this by becoming the class clown. He was an energetic prankster who got attention the old-fashioned way—he earned it! He stole CDs, sold parsley to a classmate as marijuana and freely passed around the Internet pornography he downloaded.

Carneal was hardly a gun enthusiast, and friends noticed no pronounced interest in violent movies, music, TV or video games. The media had spread the notion that he was inspired by the movie *The Basketball Diaries,* in which a character played by Leonardo DiCaprio walks into a classroom and blows away several students with a shotgun. But Michael called the movie "boring" and said, "I don't know why it happened, but I know it wasn't a movie."[7]

He had a crush on a tall, pretty girl named Nicole Hadley. He phoned her almost nightly in the weeks before the shootings, ostensibly to discuss chemistry. Occasionally they did homework together in his home. Nicole was self-assured enough to remain a defiant brunette in a school where bottle blond was very much in vogue. But the pictures of the two of them said it all. Michael had the owlish aspect of a pubescent Steve Forbes, and Nicole looked like a model for the cover of *Teen* magazine.

Michael Carneal had not yet experienced his first kiss. When a school gossip sheet labeled him gay, he almost cried. The barbs stung. "Alone in his room, with his Internet porn for company, the lack of a girlfriend was a source of physical frustration and social embarrassment," wrote Jonah Blank in *U.S. News & World Report*. "When he fired into the prayer circle, his first bullet struck Nicole Hadley."[8]

R-E-S-P-E-C-T

Michael was insecure, self-centered and hungry for attention. He wrestled with the frustrations of puberty and the passion to be approved by his peers. These would hardly be considered traits that set him apart from millions of other teenagers across North America. His craving for respect even showed up in a secret story that was not discovered until after the shootings at Heath High.

It was the tale of a shy kid named Michael. He was picked on by the "preps"—the popular kids. The hero in the story was a big brother with a gun. He shot to death all those who had teased his little brother. Then Michael gave these corpses to his mother as a gift.

The real Michael Carneal, of course, had no such heroic sibling. There was no fictional alter ego to save him from the threat of the popular students. So he had to take things into his own hands. His best explanation for pulling the trigger is pathetically childish: "I just wanted the guys to think I was cool."[9]

Well-Hidden Demons

In his *U.S. News & World Report* article, Jonah Blank freely admits that the Michael Carneal carnage "may be the most baffling" in the 1997-98 school year of mass murders and mayhem. "Nearly every theory trotted out at the time of the tragedy now seems hollow. . . . What's striking about Michael Carneal is how ordinary he is. . . . Whatever demons may have lurked in Michael's heart remain well hidden."[10]

A psychiatric report was prepared as evidence for his trial—an evaluation by doctors who spent several days interviewing him, his family and five of his friends. What did they conclude? "Michael Carneal was not mentally ill nor mentally retarded at the time of the shootings."[11] Nevertheless, the defense was still able to use mental illness in the final plea arrangement.

Guilty but Mentally Ill

On October 5, 1998, Michael Carneal pleaded "guilty but mentally ill" for killing three schoolmates as they stood in a prayer circle. Under a plea arrangement, McCracken Circuit Judge Jeff Hines agreed to accept the plea on the condition that the maximum penalty would be imposed: life in prison without the possibility of parole for twenty-five years. Prosecutor Tim Kaltenbach said confidently, "He's definitely going to serve 25 years."[12]

When Judge Hines asked the slightly built, bespectacled Carneal, "You are fine today, in terms of your mental health?" the defendant replied, "Yes, sir." The same question was directed to defense attorney Tom Osborne. The lawyer explained that although Mr. Carneal was suffering from paranoia and a schizophrenia-like personality disorder, he did not believe these conditions were affecting the defendant's decision.

As of this writing, Carneal has been incarcerated for eighteen months. He says that he prefers the juvenile detention center to high school. He likes the food. He sleeps well. But best of all, "People respect me now."[13]

Once Again: Why?

And still the nagging question remains: Why? In the days that followed this bloodbath, folks in West Paducah were trying hard to understand this incomprehensible carnage. Principal Bill Bond said, "His father's a deacon and his sister's the valedictorian. Michael never dressed in black or wore upside-down crosses. He does not fit the mold of what our society says an angry person should be like."[14]

U.S. News & World Report summarized and quickly dismissed the following theories:

- Cinematic inspiration: Parallels to Carneal's viewing habits make this hard to justify.
- Outcast's revenge: Carneal never claimed to have been bullied by anyone.
- Firearm frenzy: Prior to the slaughter, he had never handled a gun in his life.
- Assault of atheism: Carneal had accepted confirmation in May of 1997 at a Lutheran church and was a regular churchgoer.[15]

In fact, everything about this incident points to the fact that Michael Carneal knew exactly what he was doing on December 1, 1997. He created an elaborate plan to get noticed by shooting his classmates and then he carried it out. It was a deliberate act. It was carefully designed. Malice aforethought. Something deep inside this fourteen-year-old wanted to kill and injure. We simply must find out what is going on here. This crime spree had nothing at all to do with Carneal's "nurture"—it was most certainly a problem with his "nature."

Gwen Hadley, mother of Nicole, one of Michael's victims, offered this grim and prophetic comment: "It's going to happen again. This can happen anywhere, at any time."[16]

Indeed it did.

Next stop: Jonesboro, Arkansas.

Chapter 5

Lured into the Crosshairs

"These are cold-blooded, evil children, and I don't care how bad that sounds." [1]

—a neighbor of Arkansas
school shooter Andrew Golden

In a cogent article chronicling the assassinations in Arkansas in March, 1998, Nadya Labi begins with these memorable words:

> . . . the news out of Jonesboro, Ark., last week was a monstrous anomaly: a boundary had been crossed that should not have been. It was news horrifying enough to cause parents all over America to wonder if they were doing enough to wall away their children from the bad angels that can steal into young souls to stifle the knowledge of good and evil. The shooters in custody . . . were two very young boys—one just 13, the other only 11. And

> now they will be tormented by more memories than if they had lived a thousand years.[2]

It was March 24, 1998.

Actually, that day started out with a laugh. At breakfast, Mitchell Johnson told his family a funny story about an elderly lady who grabbed his ear while he sang with his church youth group at a Jonesboro nursing home. The ear twist caused him to sing in a higher key. His sister, Angie, was doubled over with laughter as Mitchell went on and on. The story ran so long that he missed the school bus that morning. So he told his mother, Gretchen, that his stepfather would drive him to school.

Instead, according to plans made earlier, this thirteen-year-old drove the family's gray van over to a classmate's house—Andrew Golden, eleven. This van had been loaded in advance with food, camouflage netting, ammunition, hunting knives and survival gear. They wanted the weapons in the steel gun vault owned by Andrew's father. But even using a hammer and blowtorch, they could not gain access. So they stole the ones that were unsecured: a .38-caliber derringer, a .38-caliber snub-nose and a .357-magnum revolver.

Next, they needed gas. The boys had to stop at three service stations before anyone would let them fill the tank. Then they drove to the home of Andrew's grandfather, Doug Golden. Doug is an area technician for the Arkansas Game and Fish Commission. As soon as they arrived at grandpa's residence, they broke in, stole four pistols, three rifles and about 3,000 rounds of ammunition. Doug had referred to one of his deer rifles as "deadly accurate."

They were now ready to go to school.

About one hundred yards from the wall of Westside Middle School's gym is Cole Hill, an elevated plot of land surrounded by both gravel and blacktop roads. This is where they decided to park the van. Now they had a clear view of the playground, which was enclosed by a chain-link fence. They could find cover in three feet of sage grass, kudzu vines and an array of sapling oaks, sweet gums and acorn trees. This was the perfect sniper's nest.

Andrew Golden went inside the school and pulled the fire alarm. *Time* describes what happened next:

> Despite fleeting suspicions that it was a false alarm, the exercise proceeded. . . . The kids, a little giddy at this momentary reprieve from math and English, poured out the side entrance into the midday sun—a steady stream of energy and youth, vulnerable flesh racing straight into a trap of precocious sophistication. Pop-pop-pop. The sounds came in quick succession, and the kids laughed—mistaking the volley for firecrackers, a joke, or maybe the drama students acting out a play. . . . As Candace Porter, 11, collapsed against one of the cinder block walls of the building, another student shouted,

> "Don't worry, don't worry, it's all fake!"—to which the bleeding Candace responded, "No it's not! I just got shot!" And then the undeniable masks of pain came over the faces of the fallen.[3]

The next moments were utter chaos—bullets flying, bodies falling and children running for cover in every direction. English teacher Shannon Wright, thirty-two, bravely shielded one of her sixth-graders. Emma Pittman lived. Mrs. Wright died.

Shots continued to ring out, first methodically and then more and more rapidly, even as survivors dialed the emergency dispatcher. "There's been blood loss," reported the first caller, obviously short of breath. Escaping back into the building was not an option because the doors had automatically locked as a result of the fire drill; the murderers knew this. In less than four minutes, Mitchell Johnson and Andrew Golden managed to fire off twenty-two rounds of ammunition during their furious ambush.

The wounded: 10
The dead: 5

The obituary:
Natalie Brooks, twelve
Paige Ann Herring, twelve
Stephanie Johnson, twelve
Brittheny Varner, eleven
Shannon Wright, thirty-two

Mitchell and Andrew made an attempt to escape. But construction workers had seen smoke rising from the woods and tipped off the police. Two officers chased the boys down as they were heading for the van. They offered only slight resistance, and the police easily disarmed them of nine guns. Deputy Terry McNatt reported, "The boys didn't say anything."[4] In fact, they stayed completely silent for the entire drive to the Craighead County sheriff's office.

During their preliminary hearing the next day, March 25, they were speechless as they listened to the recitation of their crimes:

- Five counts of capital murder
- Ten counts of first-degree battery

A single night in the jail found the boys outwardly changed. Mitchell requested a Bible, a minister and "some Scripture thought." Both boys requested pizza for lunch, but it was denied. Andrew Golden began to cry in his holding cell, begging for his mother. Sheriff Dale Haas said, "He wants his mama, and he wants to go home now."[5]

Mitchell Johnson: A Profession of Faith

Seven months before the murders, in September of 1997, Mitchell Johnson found God at a youth revival meeting. According to Christopher Perry, youth minister at Central Baptist Church in Jonesboro, "He made a profession of faith and decided to accept Jesus Christ as his savior."[6]

For a while, at least, Central Baptist seemed to provide a haven. Young Johnson became a fine, upstanding member of the congregation. He delighted many of the adults with his choirboy gentility. "Yes, sir" was his standard greeting for the men. He always said, "Ma'am" when he held out a chair for a lady. Most folks thought that here was a boy who had certainly been raised right. Just two weeks before the shootings, Mitchell had joined up with another group to sing and minister at a nursing home.

He struggled, as any child would, with the divorce of his parents in 1994. There were the typical teen infatuations with girls that were sometimes rebuffed. But nowhere could any hint be found that he would ever become involved in these kinds of multiple murders. How does one go from singing for the elderly with a church youth group to maliciously massacring fellow classmates in a span of a few days?

The Golden Boy

Andrew Golden was referred to by family and close friends as simply "Drew." Santa gave him a shotgun for Christmas when he was just six years old. The home videos show this tiny tot rushing to the makeshift shooting range in the backyard. He learned to bait hooks and scope out prey with his father and grandfather. Drew even developed a taste for venison chili after a successful deer hunt. He had a keen eye, and he improved his marksmanship in two ways: at a shooting range, and at the video consoles at a local Wal-Mart and bowling alley. "Drew understood law and order," the grandfather was quoted as saying.[7]

Andrew Golden also had a softer, kinder side to him. He played trumpet in the school band and anxiously awaited concerts so that he could give the "thumbs up" to relatives who came to hear him. Many mornings Drew would be dropped off at his grandparents' home to chat and sip hot chocolate while he waited for the bus. Just days before that bloody Friday, his grandmother, Jackie, said he was on his best behavior. Accompanying her to the hair salon, he was admired for his demeanor by the astonished stylists.

Pat Golden, Drew's mother, had gone through a tubal ligation after having two children from her first marriage. But because her second husband had never had children, Pat decided to reverse the procedure and later gave birth to Drew. A friend and former colleague, Joyce Prater, said that for this reason, Andrew was a very special child to his parents. "That child is the center of their world."[8]

The Usual (Unsatisfying) Suspects

In an editorial for the *Arkansas Democrat-Gazette* entitled, "The Lost Children: What Can We Do about It?" we see a series of questions and comments that sound vaguely familiar:

> What is it about today's society that would lead children to mow down their schoolmates? Is it the violence for the sake of violence on television and in the movies? Have we immunized our kids to reality? Do they react to death in the school yard as if they were just taking target practice with tin cans? Is it because we have failed to instill a healthy respect for firearms? Every time something like this happens, the same questions are raised. And there don't seem to be any clear answers.[9]

Have you noticed how the frustration continues to pour forth in ever-increasing volume with each successive school shooting? But of all the murder scenes we have witnessed thus far, this one is the most vicious and premeditated. These boys created a shooting gallery by pulling the fire alarm. They knew that their schoolmates would not be able to run back into the building to safety because of the automatic locks. This guaranteed an optimum amount of death and destruction.

Mitchell Johnson is rumored to have said that he really didn't want to harm anybody. He just wanted to scare people by shooting over their heads. But relatives of two of the fatalities vehemently disagree. Mitch Wright, the husband of the teacher who was killed, said, "He shot five times. He hit five people. He wasn't shooting over their heads."[10]

Wright also attacked the argument about the age of the killers. "It doesn't matter to me that these were boys. Their age has nothing to do with the fact that they murdered my wife and four others. Kids do things on the spur of the moment. What these boys did was not a spur of the moment thing."[11]

Tina McIntyre, mother of the late Stephanie Johnson, pointed out that "His rifle had a scope. He hunted her down like an animal."[12]

The deliberate nature of this hellish crime is both disgusting and overwhelming.

Consequences or the Lack Thereof

Mitchell Johnson pleaded guilty to five counts of capital murder at his August 11, 1998 adjudication hearing in Jonesboro. The defense for Andrew Golden attempted to use an insanity defense. But Circuit Judge Ralph Wilson Jr. of Osceola wisely refused that defense and found Andrew guilty of capital murder. Johnson and Golden are now incarcerated in the Alexander Youth Services Center in Bryant, Arkansas. But there was a complication with their ages.

> Under [Arkansas] state law, Mitchell Johnson, 13, and Golden, 11, will not face the death penalty. They will not spend the rest of their lives in prison. In fact, they are likely to be out of prison at age 18. In Arkansas, children under 14 cannot be tried as adults, and juveniles face a maximum sentence de-

> scribed by state law as "indeterminate," which means not to exceed their 21st birthday. . . . [M]ost children are released at age 18 because the state does not have the facilities to hold them longer.[13]

Governor Mike Huckabee promised that the state would either build or locate a facility to hold Andrew and Mitchell until they are twenty-one.[14]

As it stands now, Andrew Golden and Mitchell Johnson may be free in a few years. But the family members of their victims must cope with a life sentence. They will be locked up in a prison of painful memories until the day they die.

Relatives of two of the victims have filed a lawsuit against the parents of the two convicted killers as well as the manufacturers of the two guns used in the attack.[15] Though the outcome of this trial is uncertain, it is easy to understand why these loved ones are going to court. There is no sense of justice with the perpetrators behind bars for just a few more years.

In March of 1999, the *Arkansas Democrat-Gazette* did a "one year later" article on Tina McIntyre. Her daughter, Stephanie, was killed by Mitchell Johnson. Kenneth Heard reported,

> McIntyre's home is a shrine to Stephanie's memory. Angels are scattered throughout the living room. Framed prayers from people across the country hang on the walls. Stephanie's seventh-grade desk sits in the entryway. . . . "Steph was more than just my

> daughter," McIntyre said. "She was my best friend. They tell me I need to accept her death. I know she's dead, but how do you accept what happened?"[16]

Will the Real Shooters Please Stand Up?

An editorial cartoon captured the essence of some of the controversy swirling around the Jonesboro ambush.[17] It showed a pickup truck with an "NRA" (National Rifle Association) license plate. There was a shotgun clearly visible in the rear window. A bumper sticker on the back fender read:

GUNS DON'T KILL—CHILDREN DO

Whether you find the slogans of the NRA appalling or appealing, there is a powerful message in that bumper sticker. "Society" didn't do this. "Parents" didn't pull those triggers. "Video games" did not do the pointing and the shooting. Those children did this. In broad daylight, Andrew Golden and Mitchell Johnson shot and killed four defenseless students and a teacher in cold blood. They knew exactly what they were doing.

Once we accept that a thirteen-year-old and an eleven-year-old must be held fully responsible for these crimson-stained crimes, we can get to the really important question: Why? But if we deny their culpability in this carnage, we will go in circles like a cat chasing its tail. A perfect illustration of this can be found in an article that appeared in *Time* entitled, "Toward the Root of the Evil":

> Juvenile mass murderers. Fledgling psychopaths. Among the experts, the search for a new vocabulary is well under way. Psychologists are wary of speculating about specific causes in the Jonesboro killings—violence at home? A history of serious mental disturbance?—until a fuller picture emerges of the two boys and their circumstances.[18]

That "fuller picture" has now emerged. There was no "violence at home." There was no "history of serious mental disturbance." The article talks about "the psychological terrain that might make a kid capable of killing." But it turns out that there were no creepy skeletons in the closets of Mitchell Johnson and Andrew Golden. It's a pity that *Time* didn't bother to get back to us on this one after that fuller picture emerged in Jonesboro. But in fairness, they have nothing more to say. If those boys are not responsible for what they did and there are no other mitigating circumstances, we must have five unsolved murders on our hands.

However, I am pleased to announce that there is an answer. Those two boys are liable for those five deaths, and we can even understand "why." Please bear with me. We have two more stops: Springfield, Oregon and Littleton, Colorado.

Chapter 6

An All-American Kid

"Kip seemed to inherit something that left him angry inside. He was out of control." [1]

—Tom Jacobson, close friend of
Kip Kinkel's parents, Bill and Faith

May 21, 1998. Thurston High School, Springfield, Oregon, 7:30 a.m.

Two dead.

Twenty-five wounded.

Fifty-eight charges in connection with the fatal shootings, including:

- Four counts of aggravated murder
- Twenty-five counts of attempted aggravated murder with a firearm
- One count of attempted aggravated murder
- Numerous counts of assault, manufacture of bombs and theft of a weapon

Trisha Allen's mother, Jackie, had been terribly frightened by the rash of school massacres across the country. So on May 14, 1998, she had a heart-to-heart talk with her daughter, urging her to be careful. Trisha quickly dismissed the warning as parental melodrama. "Who in this town, in this school, would shoot at me?" she asked.[2]

One week later, she had the answer.

Trisha followed her usual routine that morning. She always went to the cafeteria for a doughnut, milk and gossip before classes started. When she stood up to discard her empty milk carton, she heard what sounded like firecrackers. When she turned around, she was looking straight into the eyes of a boy aiming a rifle just over her shoulder. It had to be a prank. But as bodies began to fall around her, it became so real that she was paralyzed with fear.

Kipland Philip Kinkel, fifteen, was the shooter. Carrying a semiautomatic rifle and two pistols, he calmly walked into the cafeteria where some 400 students were chatting and doing homework. Kip turned back and forth, spraying bullets. Before it was over, he had discharged fifty-one rounds of ammunition in less than two minutes. If it had not been for the heroism of another student, the body count would have been much higher.

Varsity wrestler Jacob Ryker, celebrating his seventeenth birthday that day, had already been shot in the chest. But he saw a window of opportunity to end the madness. Saying to himself, *Enough's enough,* he tackled Kinkel as he was reloading. Kip managed to get off one more shot from his 9-mm Glock pistol, which ripped through Ryker's hand. By this time, a group of guys had jumped on top to hold Kinkel until the police arrived. At the bottom of the pile, Kip Kinkel yelled, "Just shoot me. Shoot me now!"[3]

Two dead. Twenty-five wounded. So far.

After Kinkel was taken into custody, Detective Robert Antoine asked him about his parents. Kip told the officer that they were dead and it might be a good idea to search the house. They immediately went to the Kinkel residence in the Shangri-la subdivision ten miles east of Springfield. An operatic version of "Romeo and Juliet" played both eerily and endlessly over stereo speakers. Bill and Faith Kinkel lay lifeless in separate rooms. Bill was killed with a single shot to the back of the head. Faith was shot repeatedly.

The police also found several hundred rounds of ammunition on the living room floor, four bombs, bomb-making materials and how-to-build-a-bomb books. A large popcorn tin was full to the brim with 9-mm shell casings. Two howitzer shell casings. A hand grenade. Various chemicals used in making explosive devices. Computer discs were found containing bomb-building information.

And on the living room mantel, a Mother's Day card. It was signed, "Love, Kip."

The Day Before

On Wednesday, May 20, Mickell Young walked out of second-period study hall with Kip.

"How's it going?" Young asked.

"Not that great—my mom took my guns away," Kip replied.

"Oh, that sucks."

Kinkel replied, "It's not a problem. Something will happen."[4]

But Kip was arrested that same day for buying a stolen pistol from another student and hiding it in his locker at Thurston High School. He was suspended from school on the spot and hauled down to the police station. Kinkel was charged with possession of a firearm on school property and possession of stolen property. Kip convinced the officers that he intended no harm. He just liked guns. Oregon law does not allow a minor to be held in jail unless the cops have probable cause to believe the juvenile will turn violent. So he was released to his parents' custody.

In the last telephone call Kip's father made before he died, Bill Kinkel seemed to sense an approaching catastrophe. At 3 p.m. that day, he was speaking with Scott Keeney. Scott's son Aaron was the owner of the stolen handgun. Bill told Scott that he had tried to get the juvenile detention center to keep his son, but they refused. Mr. Kinkel had picked him up, and they were waiting for his wife to come home from her job teaching high school Spanish. Bill's last words to his friend were, "Kip is out of control."[5]

Sometime after that phone call, between 3 p.m. and 5 p.m., Kip Kinkel shot his father in the back of the head. He died instantly. Then he waited in the garage for his mother to return home and shot her several times. Faith died in the garage, but he dragged her corpse into one of the bedrooms. Kip then left the bodies in the house and spent the night in the woods. The next morning he drove the family's Ford Explorer to school and began his deadly rampage.[6]

A Wholesome Family

To friends and neighbors, the Kinkels could hardly have been a more wholesome family. They lived in a gingerbread-fringed A-frame house set in a wooded subdivision of Springfield. Bill was a vigorous fifty-nine-year-old who had retired from his job as a high school Spanish instructor. But he kept busy by teaching four evenings a week at a local community college. Faith, fifty-seven, was a nature lover and an avid hiker. She had a passion for Latin America, and she was a popular Spanish teacher at Springfield High School. Kip's parents were described by many as a caring mother and father. A family picture from a vacation in Disneyland spoke volumes. That photo was printed in newspapers and magazines across the land.

Their daughter Kristin, twenty-one at the time of the shootings, excelled at gymnastics and won a cheerleading scholarship to Hawaii Pacific University. Bill's closest friend, Denny Sperry, said that Kip was winsome in his own way. He could come across as polite, even friendly. "He was shy and quiet, and he had this big, beautiful smile."[7] But he also noted a stubborn streak going back to when Kip was just a four-year-old.

Kip Kinkel did not do well in the early years of school. Bill and Faith spent endless hours huddling with teachers and counselors to try to sort out his learning problems. Dyslexia? ADD? Prozac for depression? Tinted glasses for visual impairment? Finally, the Kinkels withdrew Kip from the seventh grade and tutored him at home for the entire year. Bill cut back on his college teaching schedule to accommodate this need but never complained about it.

With the onset of adolescence, Kip developed a fascination for guns and bombs. He loved to talk about weaponry. He begged his father to buy him a rifle, but Bill Kinkel tried his best to divert his son's attention away from such things. Then one year before the Thurston High School disaster, Bill finally gave in. He bought Kip a .22-caliber semiautomatic Ruger rifle. Mr. Kinkel's rationale was understandable: If he wants guns, he should learn how to use them safely. And perhaps this could bring about a closer father-son relationship.

But eventually Kip outgrew the Ruger. A few months before his death, Bill bought him a 9-mm

Glock semiautomatic—a large-caliber handgun used mainly by police. Scott Keeney recalls that "Kip was showing it off like you would a new car."[8] It wasn't long before Bill confided in friends that Kip was "totally obsessed" by guns. His aggression was escalating. He became uncontrollably angry when told "no." He had killed animals and threatened his parents.

On the afternoon of his arrest, Kip found his way into his father's gun cabinet. Then, in the words of *Newsweek*'s Joshua Hammer, "He took aim and fired, putting to lethal use the gifts Bill Kinkel had once believed would bring father and son together."[9]

Rehashing Irrelevant Reasons

When the news broke in Springfield, Oregon, the news magazines, newspapers and television talk shows came to life once again in a vain attempt to "understand" why a fifteen-year-old would destroy, in a barbaric frenzy, two parents who had tried their very best. Why would he also go to school and empty clip after clip of bullets into the bodies of his classmates? *U.S. News & World Report* summarized the answers given by the best and brightest minds. These were supposed to cover all the recent school shooting incidents:

- Parents, friends and teachers ignored signs of trouble
- Perpetrators felt like outsiders

- Some came from "troubled families"
- "Copycat" phenomenon[10]

But surely these are all just symptoms. Where's the disease? The Kinkels' family friend, Tom Jacobson, says, "There is no explanation for it. Young Kip was just a bad seed."[11]

Now we're getting somewhere.

James Alan Fox, a criminologist from Northeastern University, said after the Kip Kinkel shootings that there are fads in crime just as there are in food and fashion. "Years ago, it was freeway shootings and then carjackings. This year it's school yard shootings."[12]

U.S. News & World Report responded to this by saying, "That suggests schools might not be killing venues for long."[13]

Little did they know what was about to transpire on Hitler's birthday in 1999.

Chapter 7

Rage in the Rockies

"The finest kids in America pass through these halls." [1]

—Motto engraved in an arch over a hallway at Columbine High School

In early April 1999, Sara Martin was chosen to be a graduation speaker for Columbine High School in Littleton, Colorado. She had many fond memories of this school nestled in a town of 35,000 near the dusty-tan foothills of the Rockies, just southwest of Denver. She wrote: "I have loved fire drills and Tai Chi on the lawn with Mr. Kritzer's philosophy class. . . ." Then on a more contemplative note: "We're all looking for passion, for something, anything, in our lives." Sara also spoke of "the humanity and integrity that walk the halls of our very own Columbine."[2]

A few weeks later, on April 20, she was in the choir room when something very different was walking the halls. Dylan Klebold, seventeen, and Eric Harris, eighteen, prowled those hallways with guns and bombs. They had murder on their minds. Lots of murder and mayhem. It was by far the most elaborately planned series of executions and explosions of any of the classroom calamities over the past three years.

Several months before, on Eric Harris' web site, geysers of hate spewed forth in a chilling declaration of things to come. Harris said he longed to "blow up and shoot everything I can. Feel no remorse, no sense of shame. . . . I don't care if I live or die in the shootout, all I want to do is kill and injure as many of you [expletive] as I can. . . ."[3]

In another Internet posting on his web site, he declared, "You all better . . . hide in your houses because I'm coming for EVERYONE soon, and I WILL be armed to the . . . teeth, and I WILL shoot to kill and I WILL . . . KILL EVERYTHING!"[4]

We now know that this was no idle threat. To celebrate the birthday of Adolph Hitler, Harris and Klebold unleashed their fury in an overwhelming arsenal of bombs and bullets. After assassinating twelve students and one teacher and injuring twenty-three others, they each saved one bullet with which to commit suicide. Jefferson County Sheriff John Stone said without hesitation that this was "the worst crime I've ever dealt with in my life. It's like walking into a nightmare."[5]

Plan to Execute, Execute the Plan

Eighty investigators are now evaluating 10,000 pieces of evidence, 1,800 tips and 1,300 interviews related to this disaster. Documentation downloaded from web sites and e-mail, along with a handwritten diary, shows that the assault in Littleton had been planned over a twelve-month period. They had even determined the time of day that would yield the highest body count.

Harris and Klebold amassed an astounding munitions cadre, including:

- A double-barrel shotgun, sawed off "as much as you possibly could," according to a federal agent. This allows for the buckshot to spray widely and cause maximum damage.
- An TEC-DC9 handgun. Popular with criminals, this high-volume, fingerprint-resistant gun was one of the assault weapons banned by the 1994 Brady Bill.
- A sawed-off pump shotgun. It fires shells with BB-size pellets.
- A 9-mm semiautomatic rifle. It fires ten rounds at once.
- A propane tank bomb. This twenty-five-pound gas tank was rigged with an egg timer and a fuse. Placed in the kitchen, it was positioned to blow up a sizable part of the school. It was never detonated, but there is evidence that Klebold

and Harris shot at the tank to set off the explosion.

- Pipe bombs. More than fifty of these "very basic bombs" were found. The cylinders were packed with gunpowder, nails and broken glass—to be more lethal. Material about how to build pipe bombs had been accessed from the Internet. Evidence from the crime scene indicates that the killers followed these directions meticulously.[6]

In the minutes before their attack on the high school, the gunmen cleverly used timers to set off two diversionary bombs—one four miles away, the other two miles away. This was to confuse and delay police and firefighters responding to emergency calls from Columbine. Each bomb, disguised in a backpack, was based on two sixteen-ounce camp-stove-size propane tanks. Eyewitnesses said that the bombs sent up two successive fireballs, each forty feet high and seven feet in diameter.[7]

If Eric Harris and Dylan Klebold had completely fulfilled their master plan, the death and destruction would have been much worse. They envisioned murdering as many as 500 students, followed by random attacks on neighboring homes. The calculating killers even contemplated hijacking a jet and crashing it into New York City where the greatest number of people could be killed at once.

The level of sophistication in the planning and premeditation of these massive crimes against humanity is staggering beyond description. The only crime these boys had committed until the Columbine carnage was breaking into a van to steal $400 worth of electronic equipment back in January of 1998. What an incredible leap—from stealing parts to slaughtering people.

No Remorse, No Shame

The most shocking aspect of these bloody events will be remembered for a long time: the casual, carefree, gleeful way in which these teens executed their peers and a teacher. *Newsweek* asked, with obvious frustration, "How did brainy kids from seemingly stable, affluent homes become killing machines without a hint of remorse?"[8]

Time pleaded for an answer to why Klebold would "follow Harris into hell on earth, laughing as they slaughtered or maimed people he knew, people he in some cases truly cared about?"[9]

Wade Frank, a student at Columbine High School, remembers how carefree the killers were in their demeanor: "Then the guy in the trench coat came down the stairs and shot the guy in the back. . . . He was just casually walking. He wasn't in any hurry."[10]

Nancy Gibbs reports that

> They were laughing, excited. "Who's next?" they said. "Who's ready to die?" The two moved through the room, calling out: "All the jocks stand up. We're going to kill every one of you." . . . They approached another girl, cowering under a table, yelled "Peekaboo!" and shot her in the neck. Anyone who cried or moaned was shot again. . . . At one point one of the gunmen recognized a student and said, "Oh, I know you—you can go." And then, "We're out of ammo . . . gotta reload. We'll come back to get you three."[11]

In his personal profile for an America Online account, Eric Harris offered this for a "personal quotation": "Quit whining, it's just a flesh wound—Kill Em AALLL!!!"[12]

Bob Herbert reports in the *New York Times*,

> The kids who opened fire on their schoolmates at Columbine were said to have been giggling as they killed. A junior named Crystal Woodman said in a television interview: "Every time they'd shoot someone they'd holler, like it was, like, exciting."[13]

The most graphic illustration of the incredibly dark, cold hearts within the Columbine killers centers around Isaiah Shoels, eighteen, one of a handful of African-American students at the school. Isaiah was spotted under a desk in the library where the bulk of the bloodshed took place.

"Hey, I think we got a n—— here," one of the killers said.

They shot him in the head and, when he crumpled to the floor, added two more bullets to his face. Surveying the splattered remains, one of the killers laughed as he said, "Hey, I always wondered what n—— brains looked like."[14] They referred to it as "awesome" and talked about getting that same bludgeoning effect with the next kill.

There are no words to describe the depths of evil inherent in this kind of giddy gore. Quite frankly, the research aspect of this project has taken a physical toll on me as a writer. I have had incredible headaches and stomach spasms as I have had to read report after report of these beastly atrocities. Tears came to my eyes on several occasions as I contemplated the real-life horror I was reading. I cannot fathom how the families of the victims can cope with such diabolical details.

Adding mystery to the madness is the suicide note from Eric Harris, claiming full responsibility for his murderous deeds and those of Dylan Klebold: "Do not blame others for our actions. This is the way we wanted to go out."[15]

Requiem for the Massacred

In an emotionally wrenching photo essay, *People* magazine catalogued the lives and loves of those who were killed at Columbine High School on April 20, 1999. Each of these teenagers was brimming with energy and potential. The teacher/coach was in his prime. What a tragic waste of precious human life.

The loss was so traumatic that 70,000 people were compelled to gather on April 25 to honor the dead in a movie-house parking lot.

Here are the victims, arranged according to age, from the youngest to the oldest:

- Steven Curnow, fourteen: Steve was a *Star Wars* buff from early childhood. He was counting the days until the May 19 release of the latest episode. The family said, "He had a smile that touched everyone. It's hard to imagine life without him."
- Daniel Mauser, fifteen: Gentle and well-mannered, Daniel wasn't afraid to hug his parents. A neighbor recalls him as a mediator: "The other kids would get upset, and he would be the in-between guy." He had put off getting his driver's license learner's permit until the summer in order to concentrate on classes.
- Daniel Rohrbough, fifteen: Dan worked at his father's electronics store; he enjoyed being around his dad. During the shootings, he held open a door so others could escape. His younger brother, Andrew, said, "I don't know how I'm going to live without him."
- Kelly Fleming, sixteen: Born with a jaw that was too small and complications that made it impossible to breathe through her nose, Kelly had struggled through life. Her father said, "She was able to see the evil in the world and

didn't know how to combat it, because she truly was a defenseless, innocent kid."

- Matt Kechter, sixteen: A straight-A student, he was a six-foot, 215-lb. offensive lineman on the varsity football team. In death, Matt was found in the library with his arms around another student. "He was protecting someone," family friend Mike Mesch said. "That was Matt."
- John Tomlin, sixteen: He was an old-fashioned kid who wore his values on his sleeve. His mother said that the world should remember "that he loved the Lord, that he wanted to live his life for Christ." His father added, "And he was a good son. He was just good."
- Kyle Velasquez, sixteen: Kyle had transferred to Columbine just three months before his untimely death. A bespectacled six-footer who weighed 220 pounds, he was called by his father "our gentle giant." Father and son shared a passion for Denver's pro sports teams. "We were always together."
- Cassie Bernall, seventeen: Known as the "Columbine Martyr," Cassie was asked directly by one of the killers, "Do you believe in God?" Her response was bold: "Yes, I believe in God." She was promptly shot in the head after the shooter said, "There is no God." (See chapter 19 for more on this.)
- Corey DePooter, seventeen: April 20 was the day that Corey was supposed to go to the bank with his dad to get a loan for a used Mustang. A

condition for getting the car was that Corey had to keep his grades up. This is why he was in the library on that fateful day.

- Rachel Scott, seventeen: The third of five children, Rachel was an outgoing, committed Christian. She loved acting and did especially well in a class on forensics, a combination of public speaking and debate. She worked in a sandwich shop. Like Cassie Bernall, Rachel was shot for confessing her belief in God. (See chapter 19.)
- Isaiah Shoels, eighteen: He underwent heart surgery as a seven-month-old baby to repair a malformed valve in his left ventricle. Doctors warned that he might not live past age five. Instead, Isaiah went on to play in a youth football league and to wrestle for Columbine. He lifted weights to pack 120 pounds of solid muscle onto his diminutive 4' 11" frame. One of only sixteen African-Americans at Columbine, his father said, "Isaiah was color-blind."
- Lauren Townsend, eighteen: This 5' 11" senior was known for her graceful style and mean spike on the volleyball court. She worked at an animal shelter after school where she had a distinctively gentle way with the frisky inmates. Her own pride and joy was a Yorkshire Terrier named Bailey. Her 4.0 average earned her the President's Award for Education Excellence and membership in the National Honor Society. She was also a leading

contender to be one of the class of '99's valedictorians.

- William "Dave" Sanders, forty-seven: When he could have run for his life, Dave Sanders ran toward the gunfire. The popular business teacher and girls' basketball and softball coach saved the lives of many students by shouting warnings and giving direction to the frightened masses. He bled to death from multiple gunshot wounds while waiting for the SWAT teams to arrive. Survivors include his wife, Linda, four daughters and five grandchildren.[16]

"Scars Might Never Fade"

Two months after the carnage at Columbine, *USA Today* reported on those who were wounded in the ambush: "There were 23 who were injured and lived. They are healing on the edges of the spotlight: athletes in wheelchairs, teenagers with bullets still inside, children and adults with scars that might never fade."[17]

Four remained hospitalized sixty days after the massacre:

- Richard Costaldo, seventeen: This is the young man who was with Rachel Scott when she was martyred for her faith (see chapter 19). Richard was shot four times, and when SWAT team members dragged him away by his feet, he could not feel their hands. His spinal injuries may make it impossible for him to walk again.

- Sean Graves, fifteen: Shot four times, he was injured at the base of the spine. He has significantly diminished motor function and feeling in his legs. Dr. Burt Katubig said that Sean's healing will have to be both "physical and psychological because he was an athletic 15-year-old boy."
- Anne Marie Hochhalter, seventeen: Bullets pierced her chest and spine, which caused an immediate paralyzation from the waist down. Bullet fragments are still inside her body. Her father said, "We have to prepare for her to be in a chair. But our long-term prognosis is that we'll have another miracle."
- Patrick Ireland, seventeen: The gunmen left him partially paralyzed on his right side, along with a brain injury that affects his ability to process language. He is beginning to walk with the aid of a walker and a therapist.

Three others were released from the hospital, but face incredible challenges:

- Valeen Schnurr, eighteen, still has two bullets remaining inside of her after nine gunshot wounds to her left arm, abdomen and chest. She is also undergoing counseling. (See chapter 19 for more on Valeen's courageous stand for God.)
- Lance Kirklin, fifteen, was shot in the face. He has had a bone graft to rebuild his shattered left jaw.

- Mark Taylor, sixteen, is in and out of the hospital dealing with complications from his injuries. After surgery on his abdomen, he developed an infection and had to have another operation to drain a lung. He is scheduled for a hernia operation too.[18]

Columbine Copycats

The weeks that followed the deadly rampage in Littleton were littered with dozens of potential copycat incidents across North America. *Time* reports, "Authorities rounded up scores of kids for allegedly plotting to blow up their schools, sneaking guns onto campus or threatening to off their enemies. Some schools hired guards; others canceled classes altogether."[19]

I briefly mentioned the first occurrence of murderous imitation in chapter 2. It was just eight days after Columbine. Sporting a three-quarter-length parka, a fourteen-year-old boy sauntered toward the doors of W.R. Myers High School in Taber—a small town in the Canadian province of Alberta. Someone with a smirk on his face asked, "Do you have a gun under there?" Indeed he did. Moments later the ninth-grade dropout whipped out a .22-caliber rifle, killing a seventeen-year-old boy and critically wounded another.[20]

Consider some other copycat attempts:

- Four fourteen-year-old boys were arrested in Wimberley, Texas on April 23 for allegedly planning to blow up their junior high school. The plot was initiated well before the Colorado massacre, but no doubt the Littleton tragedy spurred fellow students to report the boys after overhearing them bragging. Bomb-building instructions (downloaded from the Internet) and gunpowder were found in a search of the perpetrators' homes. The four eighth-graders (pause a moment to let that school grade sink in) were charged with conspiracy to manufacture explosives and commit murder and arson.[21]
- A school in Hillsborough, New Jersey was shut down for a day when students received e-mail warnings: "If you think what happened in Colorado was bad, wait until you see what happens in Hillsborough Middle School on Friday."[22]
- In Bakersfield, California, authorities yanked a thirteen-year-old boy out of school after classmates spotted him loading a .40-caliber handgun. He had a hit list of thirty names with "they deserve to die" scrawled at the bottom.[23]
- Bomb threats forced evacuations in seven Detroit schools.[24]
- In rural Weyauwega, Wisconsin (100 miles northwest of Milwaukee), schools had to be evacuated for two days in a row because of threatening notes that were found.[25]

- Three times in one week, many of Washington D.C.'s 71,000 students were sent home because of bomb threats.[26]
- In Fairport, New York, near Rochester, the police confiscated gunpowder, propane and bomb-making books at the home of a twelve-year-old sixth grader. He had been plotting for some time to blow up his middle school.[27]
- Four Michigan boys were charged with plotting a shooting at their middle school similar to the rampage in Littleton. Justin Schnepp and Jedaiah Zinzo, both fourteen, were arraigned for conspiracy to commit murder in a plan to kill classmates during a school assembly at Holland Woods Middle School in Port Huron, Michigan. Two others, ages twelve and thirteen, have been charged as juveniles for the same crimes.[28] St. Clair County Assistant Prosecutor Michael Wendling said, "This was to be a Colorado-style shooting and bombing. The goal was to kill more people than in Columbine."[29] The elaborate plans included holding up a gun store to amass an arsenal of weapons. They would then descend on the school and force the principal at gunpoint to call an assembly.[30] Then the boys planned to rape some of the girls and kill a large number of classmates. They had drawn up a hit list of 154 people and stolen a building plan from the custodian's office.[31]
- One month to the day of the Littleton murders, Thomas "T.J." Solomon, fifteen, walked into

> Heritage High School in Conyers, Georgia, armed with a .357-magnum pistol and a .22-caliber rifle and began shooting students in the commons area. For a moment afterward, he contemplated suicide but changed his mind. Stacey Singleton, seventeen, a junior at Heritage, said, "When he started shooting, he had the biggest look of hatred I've ever seen." May 20 was also the last day of classes for seniors.[32]

Perhaps the most disturbing aspect of these copycats is that they appear to be competing with the Columbine killers—"We can kill more than they did!" It's become a pinball game of sorts where the next guy up tries to score more points. Unfortunately, this is no silly game. Human lives are at risk.

As much as I abhor saying it, there may be more—much more—death in our schools. Dark forces were unleashed in Pearl, Paducah, Jonesboro, Springfield and Littleton. "The dark genie is out of the bottle and swims in the seas,"[33] said one writer. It will be difficult to put him back in that bottle.

Five Empty Seats at Graduation

Graduation day was May 22, 1999, for Columbine High School in Littleton, Colorado. It was a bittersweet day that was marked by the absence of five individuals who were supposed to be there.

Lauren Townsend should have been there. She had achieved a perfect 4.0 grade point average. She was one of seventeen seniors honored as valedictorians. Her older sister and two older brothers, all Columbine grads, went to receive her diploma. Her mother held up her graduation gown with its gold valedictorian sash as 8,000 people watched in utter silence.

Isaiah Shoels should have been there. His parents, who had already received his diploma, said it would be too painful to attend the ceremony.

Teacher Dave Sanders was supposed to be there too, watching his students graduate.

There were brief, dramatic pauses during the reading of the members of Columbine's graduating class of 1999:

"Jennifer Harmon . . . (pause) . . . Gabrielle Harris . . ."

"Melanie King . . . (pause) . . . Don Klein . . ."

The names of Eric Harris and Dylan Klebold would have been inserted between those students. They were scheduled to be graduating on that day too.

What an incredible, emotional day in Littleton. Three of the wounded graduated. One rolled across the stage in a wheelchair, while another limped slightly because of the soft cast on her left foot. Parents of the dead must have been wondering "what might have been." Parents of the killers must have felt indescribable guilt, shock and grief. What must it have been like for the Harrises and Klebolds to revisit those graduation announcements and party plans?

Jonathan and Stephen Cohen, students at Columbine, wrote an anthem in tribute to their school and its agony, called "Friend of Mine." At the close of the graduation ceremonies, they sang the final lines:

Columbine, friend of mine.
Peace will come to you in time.
Columbine, friend of mine.

With that, Frank DeAngelis, the principal who lost fourteen students and one faculty member, slumped in his chair and wept.[34]

In the wake of the tragedy in Colorado, psychologists and psychiatrists have suggested their own version of the "natural born killer" theory. They see it as an aberration in a small percentage of young men who are afflicted with strange disorders, enraged by some kind of genetic flaw or damaged by an abusive childhood.

Could one or more of these theories be the real reason behind these killers' unrelenting rage? Read on and see.

Chapter 8

The Science (Fiction) of Teen Violence

"The hardest thing about the search for an explanation was the growing fear that there might not be one." [1]

—Nancy Gibbs

Much of the confusion over school violence can be traced to twisted thinking about what "causes" human behavior. Simplistic "psychobabble" that seeks to blame everyone else and everything else but the perpetrator has definitely taken its toll. Much of what has been called "science" is being unmasked as "science fiction" and we are reaping what we have sown.

CNN conducted a "quickvote" Internet poll, beginning the day of the Littleton massacre. They offered a disclaimer, saying, "This poll is not scientific and reflects the opinions of only those Internet users who have chosen to participate." But here is their question and the results of the poll when I checked it thirteen days later:

Who or what is most responsible for school violence?

Kids—13% 2,434 votes
Parents—29% 5,488 votes
Schools—3% 529 votes
The Media—18% 3,290 votes
Access to Guns—14% 2,647 votes
All of the Above—19% 3,527 votes
None of the Above—5% 848 votes[2]

Time.com started a similar poll on April 26, 1999:

The Littleton Massacre

Which one of the following factors do you think is the most to blame for the Littleton school shooting massacre?

Games, Movies, TV—15.10%
Firearm Availability—13.32%
Parents—37.05%
Police—6.21%
School Officials—5.62%
"Goth" Culture—3.92%
Random Evil—18.46%[3]

According to both polls, parents are the scapegoat *du jour*. But note that neither survey dared to include a simple category like "The Shooters Themselves." The moral and ethical thinking in our culture has been poisoned by the notion that "there's got to be someone else to blame." *USA Today* had a story in the "Life" section on May 11, 1999, entitled, " 'We're all responsible' for youth violence." President Clinton had conducted a White House Strategy Session on Children, Violence and Responsibility the day before. Said the President, "We are not here to place blame, but to shoulder responsibility."[4]

With each successive school massacre, the drum beat is getting louder for answers and solutions. Psychologists, psychiatrists, biologists and youth social workers are getting their "fifteen minutes of fame" on TV talk shows. They are being interviewed on all the major news networks. The experts are speaking out in newspapers and major weekly magazines like *Time*, *Newsweek* and *U.S. News & World Report*. They are appearing on *Dateline, Nightline, 20/20* and *48 Hours*.

Troubled Relationships and Temperamental Difficulties

Dr. James Garbarino is the professor of human development at Cornell University and the noted author of *Lost Boys*. His theory is that in a toxic world, there are children raised in such misery that they would naturally be moved to repay the world with violent acts. On May 4, 1999, he was asked how he would explain the two killers in Colorado who, by all appearances, suffered no serious disadvantages? His initial reaction was this:

> At first it looks inexplicable, if they don't seem to have the history of troubled relationships and temperamental difficulties. But as the days proceed and these boys' lives are put under the microscope, we may begin to see a pattern of early difficulties.[5]

One week later, it was becoming more apparent that there simply was no "pattern of early difficulties." Dr. Garbarino made some adjustments in his explanation:

> What "poverty" is really about is a feeling of deprivation or shame that you don't have what other people have. It's a feeling of unjust deprivation. These boys in Colorado certainly felt poor in the sense they didn't have the acceptance of their peers that they needed or wanted. They felt that was unjust, that they weren't getting what they were entitled to.[6]

But this is an evasive, irrelevant and totally unsatisfying answer to the foundational question. In no way could it explain the slaughter of thirteen human beings. Writing for *USA Today*, Kathy Kiely and Gary Fields marvel at how "normal" these boys appeared to be:

> Despite all the evidence of strange behavior by Harris and Klebold that has surfaced since the killings, many aspects of their lives seemed just plain normal. So normal that now, after almost two weeks of public outrage about warning signs that many say were ignored by the parents, school officials and police, more and more friends and

> classmates of the two gunmen say that no one could have seen it coming.[7]

There is a strong pull to immediately label Harris and Klebold "homicidal maniacs." Terms like "inhuman," "subhuman" and "animal" have pervaded articles about the shootings in an apparent attempt to ameliorate the national agony. The kind of hardhearted nihilism that pervaded these shootings seems to call for another species. Even Dylan's mother, Susan Klebold, told her hairdresser with tears flowing down her cheeks, "This monster was not the son I knew."[8]

Nevertheless, there is a considerable body of evidence showing how "just plain normal" these teenagers were. Everything youth experts say children need to stay out of trouble, Harris and Klebold seemed to have. Observe the following illustrations:

- Chris Hooker, an eighteen-year-old senior says, "I never saw hate in him [Klebold]." He spent hours on the phone with Dylan arguing about who is the greatest baseball player. When Hooker's brother died in a motorcycle accident in February 1999, Klebold comforted Chris by saying, "He's in a better place now."[9]
- Both boys attended a good school. Columbine is considered one of the best in the area.
- They had caring, two-parent homes. When Dylan and Eric were picked up for trying to steal a car, both of their dads came to court with them. Both boys told the judge they had

curfews: Harris' at 6 p.m., Klebold's at 9 p.m. A colleague of Mrs. Klebold told the Associated Press, "As far as I can tell, this family was utterly, utterly normal. They did everything right."[10] According to *Time*, "These were parents who came to all the Little League and soccer games. They even came to practices."[11]

- Both boys had jobs—they worked the dinner rush slot three to five nights a week at a pizza shop—and were considered reliable workers by their employer.
- Jefferson County Sheriff's Department spokesman Steve Davis said that autopsy reports showed no evidence of any kind of drugs or alcohol in the bodies of Harris or Klebold.[12]

After another "normal-looking" boy opened fire on classmates in Conyers, Georgia, Joe Watts, a senior at Heritage High School, said, "It's getting hard to know who's the psycho now."[13]

Antisocial Personality Disorder

Other experts in this field refer to "antisocial personality disorders" as the cause of adolescent violence. *U.S. News & World Report* offers these insights in an article entitled, "Exorcizing the Pain":

> Such disorders are believed to affect some 7 million Americans. On one end of the spectrum, they are barely noticeable. A child may shoplift or an adult may be abusive. At the other end, there's

> violence of the kind that convulsed Littleton. In Harris's Internet writings, University of Iowa psychiatrist Donald Black finds signs typical of the dark end of the spectrum. Among them: a sense of superiority, a lack of remorse, no conscience, disregard for others, and the need for revenge. "It's a myth that behind any horrific act like this there must be some kind of longtime trauma or abuse," says Black, the author of *Bad Boys, Bad Men*. "Most antisocial children I treat have pretty normal parents and pretty ordinary home lives."[14]

According to this definition, Harris and Klebold most certainly had an "antisocial personality disorder." Had they not committed suicide, I am quite confident that Dr. Black or some other psychiatrist would have been a witness for the defense along these very lines. But I would point out that no one among us could say that we have never experienced:

- Feelings of superiority
- A lack of remorse for some wrong action
- A lack of conscience with regard to an evil word, deed or thought
- A disregard for others
- A need for revenge

Does this then imply that we are all afflicted with antisocial personality disorder at one time or another in our lives? The brush Dr. Black is painting with is much too broad. The distinguishing characteristics of the personality disorder theories are so commonplace that any perverse behavior could be swallowed up in their enormous embrace. It may sound clinically clean and tidy, but its very tidiness is why it cannot possibly account for the twisted, bloody massacres around the nation. Thomas L. Friedman put it this way:

> Littleton has gone to a very deep place. It's not hard to understand why. The shootings in Littleton were not by deprived youths, and they were not carried out by an obviously depraved single gunman, who could be written off as a psycho. Rather they happened in a "Leave It to Beaver" neighborhood—and the gunmen were Wally and Eddie Haskell.[15]

Wanted: Brain Surgeons

Newsweek weighed in with an article entitled, "Why the Young Kill." This came complete with actual photos of brain scans from sixteen-year-old boys. They reported:

> Science has a new understanding of the roots of violence that promises to explain why not every child with access to guns becomes an Eric Harris or a Dylan Klebold, and why not every child who feels ostracized, or who embraces the Goth esthetic, goes on a murderous rampage. The bottom line: you need a particular environment imposed on a particular biology to turn a child into a killer.[16]

We are told that boys who have divorced parents are susceptible to become violent unless they find another source of unconditional love. This is because ". . . such boys fail to develop, or lose, the neural circuits that control the capacity to feel and to form healthy relationships. That makes them hypersensitive to perceived injustice."[17]

The article strongly hints that certain young people are "biologically vulnerable" and that certain young brains may be "predisposed to violence." However, Dr. Adrian Raine, psychologist from the University of Southern California, comes right out with it:

> There is clearly a biological predisposition to violence. We know there are murderers who don't have the usual signs—a history of child abuse, poverty, domestic violence, broken homes—and yet they commit violence. Research suggests the cause may lie internally, in terms of abnormal biological functioning.[18]

But if we blame these murders on bad genes, how can one explain the well-adjusted siblings that came from the same parents? The notion that brain chemistry is predetermined or can be altered by environment in such a way as to produce killers is baseless and ludicrous. This is unbridled hyperbole rather than hypothesis. And it is just another attempt to get away from the issues of evil and personal responsibility. Writing in the *Chicago Tribune*, Leonard Pitts Jr. puts in writing the overwhelming frustration of blaming culture, media, parents, genetics, et. al., for what happened at Columbine High School:

> All of it explains. None of it truly answers the question that burns like fire and haunts like spirits: Why? . . . The urge to slap a label upon this horror, to box it up and store it away, is strong. But ultimately what happened in Littleton is larger and more monstrous than easy answers allow for. In the meticulousness of the planning, in the viciousness of the attack, in the giddy "gladness" with which the mission was carried out, it seems to mock our attempts to understand.[19]

Prozac to the Rescue

Time did several follow-up articles on the Columbine and Conyers shootings, which they called a special report on "Troubled Kids." A large portion of this segment dealt with the alarming rise of depression among adolescents. The implication was that despair could have been the driving force behind the various school shootings. Psychiatrist David Fassler was quoted as saying, "Depression occurs in children more often than we realize."[20]

The article, "Escaping from the Darkness," went on to say just how difficult this teen despondency is to define:

> Depression is slightly harder to diagnose in adolescents than in adults, and not because teens are expected to be moodier and more withdrawn.

> They are less likely to realize that they are depressed and thus less likely to seek help.[21]

This statement requires special interpretive skills. *Kids who are depressed don't even know it? We can only discover their despair when they come to school with bombs and guns?* Without callously dismissing those cases of genuine teenage depression, I submit that this excuse for adolescent rage is perversely exaggerated. It is impossible to look at the case studies presented in this book and then write off the bullets and bloodshed to despondent young people.

Depression is a normal part of adolescence. Rapid changes in physical growth, intensified hormone production, passion for peer approval and a host of other forces combine during the teen years to produce many dark days. This is simply too common to qualify as the answer to why kids kill. If every adolescent who had ever been depressed resolved their despair with guns and bombs, the carnage would leave very few teens alive.

Journalists with an Edge

In the wake of the Columbine killings, I notice a growing "edge" to the TV, newspaper and magazine interviews. The talk-show hosts, news anchors and writers are becoming impatient with the so-called experts. The blame game is shifting.

There is a mountain of evidence to suggest that Eric Harris and Dylan Klebold came from caring, affluent families. In no way do they fit the profile of other mass murderers. There is something very different going on here: no history of abuse; no drugs or alcohol; no mental illness. Evidently, relatively normal teenage boys just decided to go on a killing spree. Modern psychology and psychiatry simply cannot deal with this morbid reality. This is way out of their league.

In a poignant editorial the day after the murders in Jonesboro, Arkansas, "What Is There to Say?," this frustration came pouring forth in the *Arkansas Democrat-Gazette*:

> We cannot think of anything to add this morning to the sick feeling, the tears, the grief that is like fear, which all of Arkansas feels now. We are so, so sorry. So mystified. We cannot even think of what to pray, except "Oh, God!" We look at the bank of televisions in the newsroom and see our own children's faces in the place of those on the screen, and are wordless.[22]

Stone Philips offered a profile of the Columbine gunmen, Eric Harris and Dylan Klebold, on his "Weekend Magazine" program. He concluded with these unsettling words:

> Very often, boys who become violent come from broken homes, usually without a father. And that's another reason why Eric Harris and Dylan Klebold remain such mysteries. They did not come from bro-

> ken homes. A friend of Dylan Klebold's parents said they, quote, "Did everything right." As for Eric Harris, he played little league as a child, and a former teammate remembers his parents coming to every game. He says Harris's dad offered every boy who came to the plate, quote, "A pat on the back and a little confidence."[23]

Frank Pelligrini probably speaks for many journalists and citizens in his sarcastic response to the President's one-day conference on youth violence following the Columbine catastrophe. In an article for *Time* entitled, "Littleton's Nobody's Fault—It's a Disease!" with the subtitle "Caught between Hollywood and the NRA, President Clinton settles on a blame-free White House symposium," he says:

> He's got a better idea, a way to get to the head of the class on Littleton without upsetting anyone who can make him regret it. He's declaring youth violence a disease. The confab's main product . . . is the kickoff of a new surgeon general's study of violence in America. . . . Maybe they'll advise us to quit.[24]

These journalists have an edge for a very good reason: The answers offered by the various specialists and experts are completely unsatisfactory. We desperately want to know why kids kill—in language we can easily understand.

The various attempts to explain the Columbine, Jonesboro and other school shootings have centered on what made these teen murderers somehow "different" from the rest of us. I think we are asking the wrong question. In Part 2 of this book, I want the reader to clearly comprehend what I have been hinting at throughout the last several chapters. It is simply this: *All of us are natural born killers.*

Read on, won't you?

Part 2

Natural Born Causes

"Those two kids [Eric Harris, Dylan Klebold] were just rotten to the core." [1]

—Rush Limbaugh

Nancy Gibbs wrote an excellent article in *Time* entitled, "Noon in the Garden of Good and Evil." She talks about how the Littleton shootings have changed the conversation that normally transpires after such atrocities:

> The Columbine tragedy didn't start out as a front-page story about the battle between good and evil. But it has been moving there, as the trauma overflowed the argument about guns and culture and spilled into other realms. This owes in part to the fact that the massacre occurred square in the heart of America's evangelical community—Colorado is home to the Promise Keepers, James Dobson's Focus on the Family and vast and grow-

> ing megachurches—and so from the beginning the reflex was to look not for reasons but for meaning. All eyes first fell on the killers, and the questions we can neither avoid nor answer. The talk-show rituals of absolution—blame the culture, the parents, the guns, the video games—left too much unresolved for those inclined to declare that the boys were simply, deeply wicked.[2]

Ms. Gibbs' comments lead us right into Part 2. Where does evil come from? Could it be that Luke Woodham, Michael Carneal, Mitchell Johnson, Andrew Golden, Kip Kinkel, Eric Harris and Dylan Klebold were "simply, deeply wicked"? If so, how did they get that way? Were they born that way? What caused them to be evil? Or, in the words of a question in *Time*, "What turned two boys' souls into poison?"[3] Columnist Jacquelyn Mitchard put it this way: "The hate-twisted young men who brought hell to that high school in Colorado were not only strange: They were sick to the soul."[4]

What does she mean, "sick to the soul"?

And what about the rest of us who have never killed anyone and have no plans to do so—do we have the potential within us to kill? If so, where does that come from?

We find ourselves forced by the murder and mayhem in our schools to ask the bigger questions with regard to the origins of evil itself. Unless we can get to the bottom of this, there can ultimately be no satisfying answer for why kids—or anyone else—would take another human life.

Then, in Part 3, we must ask, how can those who are evil become good? Is there any hope?

So join me in a journey into the origins of evil.

Chapter 9

The Cause of Causes

"There is no man so good, who, were he to submit all his thoughts and actions to the laws, would not deserve hanging ten times in his life." [1]

—Michel de Montaigne

The Hebrews had a way of expressing "the ultimate." Their method was extremely simple. They used the same word twice with "of" in between. For instance, The Song of Songs, written by Solomon, is "the ultimate song." It is the very best. The King's letters to his beloved had no rival.

In our world, some might say that Microsoft's Bill Gates is the computer genius of computer geniuses. Others might announce that Ben and Jerry's is the ice cream of ice creams. Someone else might argue that Mercedes Benz is the automobile of automobiles.

The subject of this chapter is "the cause of all causes." I want my readers to understand the root cause of evil in simple, everyday terms. This cause has no rival. It is the original cause, and everything that is wrong about our world today finds its basis in this one reality.

Natural Born Sinners

> Now the serpent was the shrewdest of all the creatures the LORD God had made. "Really?" he asked the woman. "Did God really say you must not eat any of the fruit in the garden?"
>
> "Of course we may eat it," the woman told him. "It's only the fruit from the tree at the center of the garden that we are not allowed to eat. God says we must not eat it or even touch it, or we will die."
>
> "You won't die!" the serpent hissed. "God knows that your eyes will be opened when you eat it. You will become just like God, knowing everything, both good and evil."
>
> The woman was convinced. The fruit looked so fresh and delicious, and it would make her so wise! So she ate some of the fruit. She also gave some to her husband, who was with her. Then he ate it, too. At that moment, their eyes were opened, and they suddenly felt shame at their nakedness. So they strung fig leaves together around their hips to cover themselves. (Genesis 3:1-7)

If no one has ever done so before, allow me to introduce you to your spiritual parents. If you traced your family tree back far enough, you would discover that they are your physical mom and dad too. Yes, I'm talking about Adam and Eve. We need to take a careful look at these first humans and their response to temptation. That decision has influenced everyone and everything since the beginning of time.

The devil is introduced as one smooth operator. Note the questioning tone right up front to plant a seed of doubt in Eve's mind: *Really? Did God really say . . . ?* The implication is quite obvious: *I can't believe God would make a ridiculous request like that, can you?* There was even a little lie thrown in there to get emotions stirring. Lucifer implied that the Creator had banned all fruit. *Have fun with your fast, Eve!*

This produced the desired response. The first lady jumped on the serpent's exaggeration immediately: "No, it's not like that at all! In fact, we are free to eat from every tree but one." Eve was desperately trying to hold on to a semblance of independence. There were lots of other things that could be eaten. Lots of "yeses"—only one "no." Not too bad when you get right down to it.

Then Satan moved in for the kill. *I know you've heard God's explanation for not touching that very attractive tree there in the middle—but I want to let you in on a secret. The real reason is this: your Creator knows that if you get a nice big bite of that particular fruit, you will become His rival. You can know everything there is to know about good and evil. You can become just like God.*

We can almost picture Eve turning to Adam at this point with her eyes wide open. *Did you hear what that nice serpent said? This is our ticket to complete independence. I don't know about you, but I really like the idea that I can become just like God! What have we got to lose? I'm going for it!*

And she did. And he did. And at that moment, the human race inherited a fallen nature, which has a propensity to rebel against the will of our Creator. Just like our mama Eve and papa Adam, every one of us has this independent streak. We desperately want to live apart from God's loving controls and commands. Though He created us to be dependent upon Him, and He has every right to call the shots for each of us, we resist the reality of our subordination to God with every atom of our being. C.S. Lewis puts it this way:

> What Satan put into the heads of our remote ancestors was the idea that they could "be like gods"—could set up on their own as if they had created themselves—be their own masters—invent some sort of happiness for themselves outside God, apart from God. And out of that hopeless attempt has come nearly all that we call human history—money, poverty, ambition, war, prostitution, classes, empires, slavery—the long terrible story of man trying to find something other than God which will make him happy.[2]

This is what theologians call the principle of "original sin." The very origin of evil can be traced to the Garden of Eden on that fateful day when Adam and Eve chose to be self-dependent instead of God-dependent, self-centered instead of God-centered. Every wicked thing happening in our world today has its roots in this original failure: "When Adam sinned, sin entered the entire human race. Adam's sin brought death, so death spread to everyone, for everyone sinned" (Romans 5:12).

Though it is ultimately ridiculous to question God's ways, some have asked, "Why did He create beings who were capable of choosing rebellion? Why didn't God just create humans who were set on 'obedience autopilot'?" My father used to tell a story that I think explains why the Creator gave us this incredible right to choose.

A man had two sons. He wanted them to be loving and obedient boys. So he sent them to a hypnotist who programmed them to be model children. When they returned from their hypnotic therapy, they cleaned their rooms and made their beds everyday. Before they left for school, they always said, "I love you, Dad." When the father came home from work, they brought him his newspaper and slippers. They hugged him and again said, "I love you, Dad." Indeed, they were exemplary sons.

The experiment was successful for a while. But eventually the father became frustrated with the fact that his boys were merely behaving as they had been programmed to conduct themselves. It was impossible for him to know if they truly loved him and wanted to do their chores. Eventually the hypnotist was called back to reverse the process so that his sons were once again free to choose. And though the boys did not always clean their rooms or make their beds, it was more satisfying when they did. They did not say "I love you" as often, but when they did it was meaningful because they did so of their own free will.

The inborn tendency of human beings to do wrong is described throughout the Bible:

- "Now the LORD observed the extent of the people's wickedness, and he saw that all their thoughts were consistently and totally evil." (Genesis 6:5)
- "Man . . . is vile and corrupt, [and] drinks up evil like water!" (Job 15:16, NIV)
- "All have turned away from God; all have become corrupt. No one does good, not even one!" (Psalm 53:3)
- "All of us have strayed away like sheep. We have left God's paths to follow our own." (Isaiah 53:6)
- "For all have sinned; all fall short of God's glorious standard." (Romans 3:23)
- "We were born with an evil nature." (Ephesians 2:3)

It is quite clear that our society has a difficult time accepting the fact of our innate iniquity. Kristine Holmgren, a writer from Northfield, Minnesota, offered this shocking response to the tragedy in Littleton, Colorado:

> The young men of Minnesota don't scare me. This is Minnesota. What happened in Kentucky, Arkansas, and Littleton can't happen here. There. I said it. So, hold me accountable for my arrogance if you must. But it is wrong to hold a generation of young men accountable for the horrific actions of a few. Many of our boys may be foul-mouthed, poorly groomed, inarticulate. We may call them lazy because they watch too much television and refuse to take out the garbage. Some might be twisted because of too much and too early exposure to sex and violence. A few may even be dangerous. But that does not make all our boys evil.[3]

I certainly agree that we should not hold all teenagers responsible for the actions of those boys who have viciously slaughtered their classmates and teachers. However, Ms. Holmgren is very wrong about one thing: all the boys in Minnesota are evil. So are all the girls. And the adults. The potential for school shooting is just as high in Minnesota as it would be anywhere. Why? Because human nature is sinful. We have a bent toward wicked behavior.

This can be easily illustrated with little children. Put fifteen of them in a room with, say, one toy for every three or four kids. It won't be long until adults will need to break up fights all over. Why does this happen? Who taught them to be selfish and unwilling to share that doll or truck? No one had to teach them. They were born with a predisposition to say, "That's mine—you can't have it!"

Diane Sawyer conducted a test with children and guns for a segment on *20/20.* A clinical psychologist was the mother of a beautiful four-year-old, Michael. She had carefully taught him not to play with guns, and to tell the truth. When a policeman spoke to this group of children, her boy was the first to raise his hand and say, "Children should not play with guns." But Ms. Sawyer wanted to see what he would do in a room with just one other boy his age, several toys and a few real, but unloaded guns. It was all secretly videotaped.

When they played the video, both boys went for the guns and pretended to be shooting each other. Asked if he had played with the weapons when he came out of the room later, the boy lied directly to his father. Both parents expressed shock that their son would not only play with the firearms, but then lie about it afterward.[4]

This was supposed to be a piece about the danger of keeping guns around little children. But it revealed much more than that. This lovely child, raised in an affectionate, upper-class environment, was still insubordinate and dishonest. He did not just learn these things by watching television or being with the wrong kids. This disobedience and deceit were a part of this boy's nature at birth.

Every one of us is born with an evil nature. This is an inescapable reality. There are no exceptions among us. That book from the '70s was all wrong. I'm not OK and you're not OK. To answer that question from *Time:* sin turned those two boys' souls into poison. It will do the same to each of us if we don't get divine help (see chapter 17).

In a frightening reality check, psychiatrist Robert Coles says:

> Psychology cannot explain the enormous variations of behavior including the fact that millions of kids listen to the same rock music or see the same videos that Harris and Klebold did and never commit murder. The greater mystery really is that most people don't act this way.[5]

The Sin Nature in Eric Harris and Dylan Klebold

How does all of this relate to the tragic events at Columbine High School?

We can see many similarities with the original sin of Adam and Eve. Just like the first humans, these teenage boys wanted to be independent of everyone and everything. Harris and Klebold wanted to be in total control. No athlete or authority figure would dare stand in their way. One can only imagine the depraved rush of adrenaline that came over them as they roamed the hallways with their guns and bombs, hell-bent on destruction.

As they stood over their helpless victims, they were saying in essence, "I will be like God." Eric and Dylan yearned to stand in the place of God as they decided who would live and who would die on April 20, 1999. They longed to feel the power of the Creator Himself as they trashed the school building with gunfire and explosions.

The Simon Wiesenthal Center, which tracks Internet hate groups, examined a copy of Harris' web site. Eric had customized a version of the bloody shoot-'em-up video game "Doom." His version had two shooters, each with extra weapons and unlimited ammunition, and the people they encountered were defenseless. One Internet investigator made this poignant comment: "They were playing out their game in God mode."[6]

We should remember that murder was the last sin these boys committed, not the first. Indeed, the other transgressions led to the final bloody act. They were consumed with jealousy and envy over the status of the "jocks" at Columbine. Klebold and Harris were filled with pride. They experienced deep hatred for various students. All of these things came from a fallen nature and eventually led to the killing spree.

- They abused God's name.
- They didn't honor their parents.
- They murdered others and themselves.
- They stole.
- They lied.
- They coveted what others had (popularity).

As we look at this list and contemplate the horrors perpetrated by Eric Harris and Dylan Klebold, it's easy for us to feel smug about the fact that we would never do something like this. But I think God is trying to say something through this catastrophe to all of us.

How Dark Can It Get?

As I was writing this chapter, the murder of three-year-old Kenny Kramer rocked the state where I live. On May 19, Harold Kramer Jr. twenty-six, was charged with second-degree murder and second-degree manslaughter in Brownsville, Minnesota. In an attempt to win back a former girlfriend, Kramer bound his own son's mouth with duct tape and wrapped him in a plastic bag. He suffocated to death. Little Kenny's body was found in the woods not far from his home eight days later when his father finally confessed.

The story initially reported as a "missing child." The beautiful face of a lovely three-year-old boy named Kenny Kramer was in our newspapers daily.

When his body was found on May 18 by FBI dogs trained to locate cadavers, the truth about the tragedy was shocking and repulsive. Radio talk shows began to discuss what would cause a man to become so pitiless. "He had to be mentally ill," many said.

I don't believe for one moment that Harold Kramer Jr. was insane. He was desperate. He was lusting for a woman he could not have. But he was not mentally impaired. Kramer just got to the place where his sin nature took complete control. Knowing exactly what would happen to that lovely child, he wrapped the tape and sealed the bag. And this is how dark it can get within human nature.

So many have waited for an autopsy on Eric Harris or Dylan Klebold that would absolve them of their horrific behavior. A chemical imbalance? A different lobe formation in their brain? There has to be something to distinguish these two boys from other seventeen- and eighteen-year-olds. But such an autopsy will not be forthcoming. Their bloody rampage is yet another illustration of just how dark human nature can become.

Why does our society have such a difficult time accepting these extreme examples of the sin nature in its lowest possible form? I think I know. It's our pride. If we can somehow convince ourselves that these brutes have warped genes or mental defects, we can continue to believe that the rest of us are just fine. But if the same sin nature is within us that is within these killers, we have a problem.

Periodically, God allows the human race to see "hatred to the tenth power." It is a blunt reminder that we too have hate in our hearts. When we see the boys who wanted to "kill all the jocks" in a jealous rage, we are forced to sadly recall our own struggles with envy and jealousy. As we observe their passion for revenge, we can remember wounds from our own past that we wanted to heal by getting even. Indeed, it is a call to humble introspection: *I have not murdered anyone—but have I hated someone?*

Murder and Hatred and the Rest of Us

In an article for *U.S. News and World Report,* Jay Tolson suggests that new explanations are needed to justify the omnipresence of evil in our society: "From the early 19th century on, Gothic literature and sensationalistic true-crime reporting attempted to satisfy that need, depicting murderers as monstrous 'others' and reassuring normal folks that they weren't like that."[7]

But according to the Bible, you and I may be more like that murderer than we would suppose. Jesus made parallel statements about killing and adultery that we need to examine:

- "You have heard that the law of Moses says, 'Do not murder. If you commit murder, you are subject to judgment.' But I say, if you are angry with someone, you are subject to judgment!" (Matthew 5:21-22)

- "You have heard that the law of Moses says, 'Do not commit adultery.' But I say, anyone who even looks at a woman with lust in his eye has already committed adultery with her in his heart." (5:27-28)

John elaborates on this theme: "Anyone who hates his brother is a murderer, and you know that no murderer has eternal life in him" (1 John 3:15, NIV).

This sets up a whole new standard for judging behavior. It's not just what you do outwardly—it's also what you think inwardly. According to the Bible, there are other, nonphysical ways to murder and commit adultery. Christ explained this further in Mark's Gospel:

> It is the thought-life that defiles you. For from within, out of a person's heart, come evil thoughts, sexual immorality, theft, murder, adultery, greed, wickedness, deceit, eagerness for lustful pleasure, envy, slander, pride, and foolishness. All these vile things come from within; they are what defile you and make you unacceptable to God. (Mark 7:20-23)

It should be pointed out right here that the murderous actions of all the school yard shooters began in the mind. From the case studies in chapters 2 through 7, it is clear that much thought went into the planning of each terrifying attack. Hours, days, months and years of evil thoughts had piled up. The hearts and minds of these boys became boiling cauldrons of envy, theft, deceit, pride and foolishness. It ultimately exploded into murder.

The alarming thing is this: we are all guilty of "mental murder" and "mental adultery" to some extent. Why? Because we have all hated and lusted. Certainly the consequences in this world are vastly different for those who act out their hatred or lust in physical ways by killing or raping other human beings. But that does not excuse those who keep and savor their anger or sexual passion on the inside.

The opening quote of this chapter from Montaigne bears repeating right here: "There is no man so good, who, were he to submit all his thoughts and actions to the laws, would not deserve hanging ten times in his life."[8]

This is why it is important to understand that all human beings are natural born killers in this sense. We have the potential within us to kill another person because of our natural born cause: we have a fallen nature that is predisposed to do the wrong thing. And even if we don't actually murder someone, we will certainly struggle with hatred and anger in our relationships with some people. A longtime friend of Tom and Sue Klebold said: "If Dylan can do this, who isn't capable of it?"[9]

The Sin Cycle

The sin nature is never static in the human heart. It always seeks to take things to the next level—from fantasy to reality. One form of evil leads to even greater wickedness. For instance, a man may think he can control his lust for pornographic magazines, but that passion creates a hunger for porn movies and videos. Then that version may give way to a desire for live striptease shows. Eventually that man could find himself frequenting massage parlors or calling escort services.

In a similar way, a person may begin with envious or hateful thoughts about someone at school or work. Those musings may lead to malicious, unfounded gossip about that person. When those false rumors come full circle, as they usually do, a confrontation is inevitable. This can lead to an angry exchange, a fight and in some cases, even murder. But there is a progression here. A few seemingly insignificant sins (envious or hateful thoughts) grow larger and larger until many people get hurt.

This is why it is so important to find the way to forgiveness and victory over our evil impulses. The sin cycle will just keep on churning until our lives and the lives of those around us are ruined. Paul describes this tragic process:

> When they refused to acknowledge God, he abandoned them to their evil minds and let them

> do things that should never be done. Their lives became full of every kind of wickedness, sin, greed, hate, envy, murder, fighting, deception, malicious behavior, and gossip. They are backstabbers, haters of God, insolent, proud, and boastful. They are forever inventing new ways of sinning and are disobedient to their parents. They refuse to understand, break their promises, and are heartless and unforgiving. They are fully aware of God's death penalty for those who do these things, yet they go right ahead and do them anyway. And, worse yet, they encourage others to do them, too. (Romans 1:28-32)

How could anyone read this passage and not see it as a line-by-line description of the last year in the lives of Eric Harris and Dylan Klebold? These boys crossed a line from which there was no return. Evil thoughts became even more evil plans. Those wicked plans turned into even more wicked actions. A violent video game called "Doom" came to life in the hallways of a real high school. The pent-up sins of pride, envy and hatred exploded onto our television screens around 1 p.m. (EST) on April 20, 1999.

The Numbing Effect of Sin

Earlier in that Romans 1 passage, Paul tells us about one of the deadliest effects of sin that has run amok: "Their minds became dark and confused" (Romans 1:21).

A "dark mind" is one that is no longer sensitive to "light." And this is the end result of the sin cycle. We become desensitized to evil. In our confusion, wrong looks right. This is how Luke Woodham could explain his rampage in Pearl, Mississippi, killing two and injuring seven, with these words: "I am not insane. I am angry. I killed because people like me are mistreated every day. I did this to show society: push us and we will push back. Murder is not weak and slow-witted, murder is gutsy and daring."[10]

Woodham had come to the place in his sin-darkened mind where he could rationalize his murder and mayhem. It made sense to him. Wrong had become right. He had no feelings for the victims or their families. He had become emotionally paralyzed by his envy and hatred. With no remorse, he pulled the trigger. Harris and Klebold could laugh and shout as they shot up and blew up Columbine High School. Why? Their minds had become dark and confused because of their sin.

The Apostle Paul talked about false teachers whose "consciences are dead" (1 Timothy 4:2). The New International Version uses the phrase "seared as with a hot iron." This is a reference to a medical procedure in which nerve endings are singed to take away pain. The result is a deadened nerve which can no longer feel anything.

It is quite possible to abuse our conscience over a period of time in such a way as to render it completely insensitive to issues of right and wrong. This is the only thing that could possibly explain how Hitler's henchmen could casually shoot Jews through the head as they slid down the chutes. It's also the only possible explanation for the remorseless bloodshed and bombing that has taken place in our schools.

Not Guilty by Reason of Insanity

Some readers might assume at this point that the Bible would never condone the insanity defense in our court system. That assumption is incorrect. There are legitimate cases where severe mental or physical impairments can lead to tragic events. This was true in biblical times too. In John 9, Jesus was asked about a man born blind:

> "Why was this man born blind? Was it a result of his own sins or those of his parents?"
>
> "It was not because of his sins or his parents' sins," Jesus answered. (John 9:2-3)

The disciples assumed that the man's blindness had to be directly tied to his own sinfulness or that of his parents. The Lord's answer must have been surprising. But it corroborates the domino effect of the original sin in the Garden of Eden. Adam and Eve's transgression unleashed a series of other consequences, and one of them was physical suffering. "You will bear children with intense pain and suffering," God told Eve (Genesis 3:16). In this sense, every birth defect and disease we are facing right now can be traced back to the first act of rebellion.

We must have compassion on those who struggle with some form of mental illness. When they commit crimes, the punishment imposed should take into consideration their cerebral limitations. And we can be grateful for those who have committed their lives to caring for these individuals in special hospitals and institutions.

How Do the Other Factors Fit In?

When you accept the biblical premise that human beings are naughty by nature, then you can begin to see how other factors fit in to the total picture of human behavior. Let's consider some of the scapegoats that have been highlighted by the school shooting epidemic and place them in the context of what we've learned thus far.

The importance of a two-parent home with loving, involved parents cannot be overstated. I will have more to say about this in chapter 12. Divorce, abuse, neglect and other problems in the dysfunctional family are the results of the sinful nature of the parents. The impact of these terrible things on children is the stirring up of their own fallen natures at an earlier age, leading them into wrong directions and behaviors. You can see how this gets exponentially worse as each generation passes it down to the next.

Some have pointed out how the vast majority of violent crimes are committed by boys and men. Scientists point to testosterone and other chemical factors that may increase the male drive to barbaric behavior. Psychologists refer to the "male macho syndrome" in our culture that encourages boys and men to bottle up their emotions. Whereas females are encouraged to talk about their feelings and cry if necessary, males get the clear message: "It's not manly to cry." My wife has worked for more than twelve years with seventh- and eighth-grade boys, and she confirms this startling distinction.

William Pollack, psychologist at Harvard Medical School, is the author of *Real Boys: Rescuing Our Sons from the Myths of Boyhood.* Interviewed on *Dateline,* he said that we put boys in an "emotional straightjacket." "We tell them, 'Be stoic, don't be emotional, stand on your own two feet.' " His point is that this kind of repression often leads to an explosion. When asked specifically about the devastation wrought by Dylan Klebold and Eric Harris in Littleton, Dr. Pollack said: "They are responsible for what they did, and we are responsible for what we have done to them."[11]

I am in agreement with Pollack's conclusion even though we probably differ on how we got there. One of the definitions of sin is "to miss the mark." I believe our society as a whole has missed the mark on the issue of manhood. We have twisted God's plan for men, and we are reaping what we have sown in the violent acts of those who finally erupt after years of keeping things to themselves. Our sinful misrepresentation of what it means to be a man has only added fuel to the fire in the fallen natures of our boys.

Though this does not excuse anyone's brutality, it is an indictment on a culture which has gotten away from God in general and His pathway to emotional health in particular.

I will look at this matter in a later chapter, but for now let me say this: there is plenty of ultra-violent, hate-filled, death-obsessed music in a world that loves to hide behind the "right to free speech." Created in the minds of sinful men and women, it will have an impact on impressionable young minds, which are already tuned into evil by their essential natures. In a sense, it is a stimulant for greater evil.

Visual and Virtual Evil

Movies, the Internet, video games and television today are filled with senseless, limitless murder and mayhem. Willful, continuous exposure to such nonstop anarchy will produce long-term problems along the lines of desensitization. The careless glee of the school yard shooters as they murdered peers and professors in cold blood is a part of the sin nature package. But visual and virtual onslaughts speed up that process.

The ultimate cause of the widespread murder and mayhem must be traced back to one simple and painful reality: we are born into sin. This is the only explanation that makes any sense whatsoever for the savage deaths and sordid destruction in Paducah, Pearl, Jonesboro, Springfield and Littleton. We battle outside because of the war going on inside. "What is causing the quarrels and fights among you? Isn't the whole army of evil desires at war within you?" (James 4:1).

The killers themselves know they are personally responsible for their crimes against humanity. Do you remember what Eric Harris said in his suicide note?

"Do not blame others for our actions. This is the way we wanted to go out."[12]

Many have said that they wished Eric Harris and Dylan Klebold would have lived if only to be able to study their minds in a search for what causes such violent behavior. But there is no need to look any further than the library at Columbine High. The best proof of cause is precisely the way they were found—dead.

"For the wages of sin is death" (Romans 6:23).

In the book *Cries Unheard,* English journalist Gitta Sereny profiled the English child murderer Mary Bell. At the age of eleven, Mary killed two younger children. Ms. Bell served twelve years in prison. She is now in her late thirties and a mother herself. She understands some of the social and psychological factors that pushed her toward the deeds—fatherless, poor, brutally abused by a prostitute mother who twice tried to kill her. But she refuses to accept any exoneration that denies her own responsibility: "Nothing can justify what I did," Bell said. "Nothing."[13]

All other rationale for these brutal acts must bow to the "cause of causes": original sin. In fact we will now see that all of the other justifications can only be seen to enhance the evil that was already present in the human heart from birth.

And though the vast majority of us will not commit heinous crimes of this sort, we do well to remember that we too have a sin problem. We may harness and hold it at the level of hateful or lustful thoughts, but the evil is the same. However, there is hope and help for all of us sinners. Good news is coming.

Chapter 10

Satanic Subversion

"The devil made me do it!"

—Comedian Flip Wilson

The late comedian Flip Wilson coined the phrase, "The devil made me do it!" He frequently used this one-liner in his stand-up routines. We smile as we read it, but is there any truth in it? Is Satan real? If so, can he "make" us do evil things? These are vital inquiries as we consider the "why" behind the murder and mayhem in our schools.

Let's review some of the references to "Satan" and "evil" we have already seen. Some of these come from journalists in our major news magazines. Others are from the parents of victims and shooters. But all of them point to the existence of an evil force in this world.

- Grant Boyette, alleged co-conspirator with Luke Woodham, was a "self-proclaimed Satanist." (Chapter 3)
- Ricky Blailock, whose fifteen-year-old daughter survived Woodham's killing spree, explained the Pearl, Mississippi murders by saying: "It's the grip of Satan. He's got a grip on this world like you wouldn't believe." (Chapter 3)
- Woodham claimed to be "haunted by demons." (Chapter 3)
- *U.S. News & World Report* spoke of the "demons" that may have lurked in Michael Carneal's heart. (Chapter 4)
- A neighbor of Andrew Golden offered her assessment of Golden and co-conspirator Mitchell Johnson: "These are cold-blooded, evil children, and I don't care how bad that sounds." (Chapter 5)
- *Time* wondered about "the bad angels that can steal into young souls to stifle the knowledge of good and evil." (Chapter 5)
- Kip Kinkel was called a "bad seed." (Chapter 6)
- Susan Klebold said of her son Dylan, "This monster was not the son I knew." (Chapter 7)
- An eyewitness of the Columbine carnage said that the shooters spoke to the students "in a cruel way. . . . It was almost like Satan was trying to talk through him."[1]

In an unusually candid interview with Brit Hume on FNC's "Special Report," journalist Fred Barnes suggested that dark spiritual forces were at work in Littleton, Colorado:

> Maybe it's something for journalists to do, and that is to look into Satanism in the United States. It's cropped up in a number of these incidents where students have shot other kids. . . . These kids were worshippers of Hitler. They were obsessed with death. They wore black—that's the only thing they wore. There's darkness and there's light. They were darkness; they were followers of Satan.[2]

Charles E. Greenwalt II responded to the evil at Columbine High with this:

> There is such a thing as absolute good and evil. All of recorded history is nothing more than the struggle between these two forces expressed through different nations, persons, and political/social movements."[3]

Satan's Stealth Strategy I

I'm not sure Satan would like Mr. Barnes' idea about journalists researching Satanism. Whereas a clear majority of Americans believe in God, many are not so sure about the existence of a real devil. And C.S. Lewis points out that this is precisely how Lucifer would want it. He would very much prefer that the masses regard him as the whim of organized religion. A vague "force" perhaps, but with no real personage. In Lewis' classic *The Screwtape Letters,* he lets us in on a conversation between Screwtape (Satan) and Wormwood (a demon):

> Our policy, for the moment, is to conceal ourselves. . . . I have great hopes that we shall learn in due time how to emotionalize and mythologize their science to such an extent that what is, in effect, a belief in us (though not under that name) will creep in while the human mind remains closed to belief in [God]. The "Life Force," the worship of sex, and some aspects of Psychoanalysis may here prove useful. If once we can produce our perfect work—the Materialist Magician, the man, not using, but veritably, what he vaguely calls "Forces" while denying the existence of "spirits"—then the end of the war will be in sight.[4]

This satanic strategy has been fulfilled in the wide dissemination and popularization of New Age philosophy and thinking. God as a sovereign Creator-Sustainer has been eliminated. People, individually and collectively, have become their own god. There is talk of the spirit world, channeling and the "latent powers of the mind." Many are dabbling in the devil's domain without even knowing it. And that's the way the enemy likes it. In this way, he becomes a "Stealth Satan."

Satan's Stealth Strategy II

However, Lucifer is not only interested in hiding his presence, power and influence. He has another agenda, which he deems just as vital to his reign of terror. It is this: Satan wants to conceal the fact that we are born with a sinful nature. And he has done an outstanding job in blinding people to this essential reality. Even respected ministers have joined in the chorus.

The basic belief in our society is that human beings are essentially good by nature. We have a "spark of the divine" within us, and if we just fan it periodically, it will turn into a wonderful Christian flame. There are exceptions to this rule as evidenced by those who murder, rape, rob banks, etc., but psychologists can offer 101 reasons why there are a few bad guys around.

The belief that human beings are basically good is the most deceptive, destructive lie ever perpetrated by the father of lies. When he can convince us that this is true, we will also believe this: we will never need God or the salvation He offers through His Son, Jesus Christ. Our essential goodness will carry us through this life and our self-made righteousness will enable us to gain entrance into heaven when we die.

There is just one problem with this philosophy. Our inner life directly contradicts the notion that we are born morally upright. We may maintain an outward set of behaviors and appearances that make us look good: we don't kill anyone, commit adultery, lose our temper in public or do any of those other big sins. But on the inside, it is quite a different story. We grapple with lust and anger. We envy what others have. We think evil thoughts about other people. You know this is true from personal experience. I do too.

The prophet Jeremiah understood the truth about our moral predisposition: "The human heart is most deceitful and desperately wicked. Who really knows how bad it is?" (Jeremiah 17:9).

So why do so many people want to believe this lie? For the same reason Eve decided to go for that forbidden fruit tree in the middle of the Garden of Eden. We want our independence from God. We don't want to admit that we have a sinful nature because that implies that we need help. This rebellious passion to work things out on our own can only lead to despair and ultimately destruction.

Satan's stealth strategies—I and II. First, convince the human race that all this talk about a real devil is religious fanaticism. Second, persuade people to believe that they are inherently good. Nice by nature, not naughty.

A Fallen Angel

Now hear this: the Bible declares that the devil is a real person. He was originally one of the highest-ranking angels in the celestial hierarchy. He may have been a cherub—not one of those pudgy babies with wings that you see on Valentine cards, but a powerful, majestic being that guards the throne of God. It seems fair to speculate that in his first state, Satan perceived the glory of God from a perspective shared by few other created beings.

But at some point in the creative process, Lucifer allowed jealousy of God and His glory to possess him. He developed an insatiable desire to have the power and the prestige of the Creator. He actually wanted to take His place. When Satan made his intentions known, he was cast out of the Divine Presence:

> How you are fallen from heaven, O shining star [Lucifer], son of the morning! You have been thrown down to the earth, you who destroyed the nations of the world. For you said to yourself, "I will ascend to heaven and set my throne above God's stars. . . . I will climb to the highest heavens and be like the Most High." (Isaiah 14:12-14)

Jesus Himself witnessed this event: "I saw Satan falling from heaven as a flash of lightning!" (Luke 10:18).

Notice the fatal steps in the Isaiah passage that led to this tragic fall:

Step One: "I will ascend to heaven" (Isaiah 14:13a)

- He expresses dissatisfaction with his created order as an angel. He wants to enter that realm of existence that is reserved exclusively for God.

Step Two: "I will . . . set my throne above God's stars" (13b)

- Lucifer voices an unholy ambition to be over his peers, the other angels.

Step Three: "I will climb to the highest heavens" (14a)

- Satan seeks the position of glory occupied by God.

Step Four: "I will . . . be like the Most High" (14b)

- The devil's ultimate objective was to challenge God's sovereignty.

It is difficult to comprehend how an angel who had experienced the dazzling grandeur of the Most High God would be willing to trade that exquisite panoramic view to become the slimy serpent in Genesis 3. But herein lies confirmation that misery loves company. We see how quickly he tried and succeeded to get Adam and Eve to fall for the same power trip: "When you eat it, [y]ou will become just like God" (Genesis 3:5).

In his book *Spiritual Warfare,* Timothy Warner adds insight into the illicit desires that drove the devil to forfeit his place in heaven:

> It may be that the fall of Satan did not occur until after the creation of man. . . . When Lucifer saw this new order of beings created "in the image of God" (Genesis 1:26, 27), his jealousy was intensified. While these new persons were created lower

> than the angels for their time on earth, they were also created with the potential for glorification.
>
> Being "in the image of God," they had the capacity for likeness to God which Lucifer as an angel did not possess.[5]

This intense jealousy went through three stages. First, Satan saw what God had and wanted it for himself. Second, the devil realized that he could never have the omnipotence, omniscience and omnipresence that the Creator possessed, and thus despised Him for it. Third, he aspired to deprive God of what He had.

We can see this same exact pattern in the school shootings. Those who felt like outsiders saw the popularity that others enjoyed and wanted it badly. But they also realized that they were never going to obtain that notoriety. A hatred began to simmer within. And finally they decided that the only way to deprive the cool kids of their status was to kill them. Though the devil didn't make them do it, we can see his hand in inspiring them to do it.

The Roles and Restrictions of Lucifer

Satan learned the hard way that there truly is only one God, and He is infinitely more powerful than the combined strength of all the angels He created. Lucifer was cast out in utter defeat, but he was also given a measure of freedom to roam the earth with other fallen angels, otherwise known as demons.

The devil is limited in that he does not have God's:

- Omnipotence—unlimited power; Satan's power is limited.
- Omniscience—unlimited knowledge; Lucifer has limited knowledge.
- Omnipresence—the ability to be everywhere at the same moment; the devil cannot personally be in two places at the same time.

Here are some of his wicked activities:

- He promotes spiritual blindness: "Satan, the god of this evil world, has blinded the minds of those who don't believe, so that they are unable to see the glorious light of the Good News that is shining upon them" (2 Corinthians 4:4).
- He stimulates disobedience: "Did God really say you must not eat any of the fruit in the garden?" (Genesis 3:1). "Then Jesus was led out into the wilderness by the Holy Spirit to be tempted there by the Devil" (Matthew 4:1).
- He arouses envy: "You won't die! . . . God knows that your eyes will be opened when you eat it. You will become just like God" (Genesis 3:4, 5).
- He encourages pride: "The Devil took him [Jesus] to the peak of a very high mountain and showed him the nations of the world and all their glory. 'I will give it all to you,' he said, 'if you will only kneel down and worship me' " (Matthew 4:8-9).

- He glorifies lying and deception: "There is no truth in him [Satan]. When he lies, it is consistent with his character; for he is a liar and the father of lies" (John 8:44b). "Even Satan can disguise himself as an angel of light" (2 Corinthians 11:14). "This great dragon—the ancient serpent called the Devil, or Satan, the one deceiving the whole world" (Revelation 12:9).
- He advocates murder: "For you are the children of your father the Devil, and you love to do the evil things he does. He was a murderer from the beginning and has always hated the truth" (John 8:44a).
- He craves destruction: "Watch out for attacks from the Devil, your great enemy. He prowls around like a roaring lion, looking for some victim to devour" (1 Peter 5:8).

It becomes quite clear that Satan does indeed play a role in these terrifying school massacres. It begins when the devil determines that he has found a willing partner in crime. Then spiritual blindness sets in. Next he pours it on by promoting the worst possible series of evil temptations:

- Be disobedient.
- Be envious.
- Be arrogant.
- Lie and deceive.
- Murder and destroy.

Ultimately each individual must choose which lines he or she is willing to cross. Many stop with disobedience. Some go on to envy and pride. Others get deep into lying and deception. The school killers discussed in this book went all the way with Lucifer's prodding to bring about death and destruction.

Were They "Demon Possessed"?

It would be difficult to say for certain that each person involved in a school yard shooting was actually "demon possessed." Many who witnessed these shocking events spoke of the intense hatred that could be clearly seen in the eyes of the gunmen. The outright laughter and mockery of the cold-blooded Columbine killers would seem to indicate that by the time they began their rampage, they were completely demonized.

This does not in any way remove the element of personal responsibility. Demons cannot possess an unwilling host. As we consider the content of the music, books, Internet sites and other materials in the possession of the various perpetrators, it becomes clear that Satan had several entry points. But whether they were in fact "demon possessed" is not as vital as our understanding of Lucifer's larger role.

Jesus would have said of these shooters: "You are the children of your father the Devil, and you love to do the evil things he does. He was a murderer from the beginning" (John 8:44).

This is a profound statement about spiritual parentage. Because of Adam and Eve's rebellion, we are by nature "children of the devil." And that is even more awful than it sounds. Paul says that people by nature are ". . . full of sin, obeying Satan, the mighty prince of the power of the air. He is the spirit at work in the hearts of those who refuse to obey God" (Ephesians 2:2).

There is only one way to get back into the family for which we were originally created. There will be more about that in chapter 17.

Commenting on the role of Satan in the school yard massacres, a pastor posted this article, entitled "Ambush at School," on the Internet. Here is an excerpt:

> By disowning God, we've disowned his protection as well, thus inviting the Evil One into our lives. How could normal kids do such things? But that's just the point—it wasn't normal kids acting on their own that committed these crimes, but normal kids who opened themselves up to an evil force beyond our imagination—and who did so with the full cooperation and approval of a society that has done the same.[6]

Is there anyone or anything that can defeat this powerful menace to society? Can a human being stand up to Lucifer? If so, on whose authority? We will need to explore the answers to these important questions in chapter 18.

Next, in chapters 11 through 16, we will examine those influences that have directly or indirectly promoted the murder and mayhem in our schools. But remember—these are not the causes for the horrible crimes that have taken place. These issues do not answer the "Why?" question.

We know why. It was not, in the words of a *USA Today* editorial, because of "some shapeless, nameless, cultural force."[7] No! Blame the shooters! Just like all of us, these boys were evil by nature. They made a deliberate choice to act on their violent, sinful impulses. As a result, dozens of students never returned home from school.

But it will still be important to examine those factors that aided and abetted fallen human nature.

Chapter 11

The Abortion Distortion

"We do have disrespect for human life. I think that can lead to our young people being cavalier toward the value of human life." [1]

—State Senator Marilyn Musgrave,
R–Fort Morgan, Colorado

In the aftermath of Littleton, many are wondering if the cultural values of North America may have contributed to the rash of school shootings. Nationally syndicated columnist Cal Thomas asks some critical questions in this regard:

> Is this the price we continue to pay for believing we could live as we wish, laugh at morality, and imagine judgment day would never come? Why should young people take life seriously when their overworked, aborting, day-care, euthanasia culture does not? Life is so cheap, relationships are so meaningless—children get the message.[2]

Could it really be true, as Thomas claims, that the devaluing of human life—specifically, the legalization of abortion—might have played a part in our recent school massacres? Let me quickly remove any hint of a doubt in your mind as to where I stand: I vigorously contend that there is a direct, undeniable connection between slaughtering an innocent, unborn baby and slaughtering innocent students and teachers at school.

The Sanctity of Life

The Bible makes it absolutely clear that life is sacred from the very moment of conception. The formation of human beings takes place in a "secret place" where only God Almighty can understand the when and the how. "God's ways are as hard to discern as the pathways of the wind, and as mysterious as a tiny baby being formed in a mother's womb" (Ecclesiastes 11:5).

This incredible life-giving process, light years beyond our most sophisticated comprehension, begins with a single nucleus. The sperm is so tiny that one million of them would fit on the head of a pin, and yet it carries half of the genetic blueprint of a full-grown human being. When united with the egg, it culminates in the miracle of a baby's birth nine months later. The psalmist did his best to describe this deep mystery:

You made all the delicate, inner parts of my body
and knit me together in my mother's womb.
Thank you for making me so wonderfully complex!
Your workmanship is marvelous—and how well I know it.
You watched me as I was being formed in utter seclusion,
as I was woven together in the dark of the womb.
You saw me before I was born.
Every day of my life was recorded in your book.
Every moment was laid out
before a single day had passed.
(Psalm 139:13-16)

God declares that human life is both established and sacred from the moment that the sperm joins with the egg at conception. In that split second, the Creator's plan for an entire lifetime is fixed. Every moment was laid out before a single day had passed.

The Constitutional Right to Life

The unborn child's right to life is not just ordained by God. It was also guaranteed at the very inception of the United States government. Consider the insightful parlance found in the Declaration of Independence:

> We hold these truths to be self-evident, that all men are created equal, that they are endowed by their Creator with certain unalienable Rights, that

> among these are Life, Liberty, and the pursuit of Happiness.

Our neighbors to the north have a similar statement. In the Canadian Charter of Rights and Freedoms, it is stated:

> Everyone has the right to life, liberty, and security of the person and the right not to be deprived thereof except in accordance with the principles of fundamental justice.[3]

It is important to observe that the U.S. statement did not say that we were "born equal." We are *created* equal. The unalienable right to life, according to our forefathers, began with God's creative process at the very moment of fertilization. The choice between giving birth and aborting the child was never supposed to be in the hands of the courts, a doctor or even the parents. It is and has always been the Creator's prerogative. The Canadian charter clearly indicates that the "right to life" is inherent for every human being.

Notice also the phrase in the U.S. Declaration, "by their Creator." The Canadian Charter begins with this statement:

> Canada is founded upon the principles that recognize the supremacy of God and the rule of law.[4]

The founders of the United States of America and Canada did not believe that the human race was an accident spawned in a primordial pool. We did not evolve into our status as Homo sapiens—we were created that way by a loving God. This, they believed, was another testimony to the intrinsic worth of each human being.

But evolution has been taught in our schools as virtual proof against the existence of God. It places in the minds of young people a subtle atheism, and it presupposes the notion of meaninglessness in the universe. This has had an enormous impact on the reduced value placed on human life. If we are just the product of time plus matter plus change, how can we say that any person has worth or significance?

The constitutional right to life in both Canada and the U.S. is founded upon the basic belief that there is a God, and that He created each of us with purpose and dignity.

Abortion North of the Border

In Canada, Section 287 of the Criminal Code became law in 1969. This made it a criminal offense to "procure a miscarriage." It stated that anyone who

> . . . with intent to procure the miscarriage of a female person, uses drugs, instruments or manipulation of any kind, for the purpose of carrying out their intention, is guilty of indictable offence and liable to imprisonment for life.[5]

The Code exempted doctors from liability if a hospital abortion committee was prepared to sign a statement to the effect that the pregnant woman's life or health was endangered.

But Canada's "doctor of death," Dr. Henry Mortgentaler, was determined to establish abortion clinics in several Canadian provinces. He forced the issue of the lawfulness of Section 287 of the Criminal Code. In 1988, the Supreme Court of Canada ruled that 287 offended Section 7 of the Charter, and that the former was of no force or effect. Chief Justice Brian Dickson said:

> Forcing a woman by threat of criminal sanction to carry a foetus to term unless she meets certain criteria unrelated to her own priorities and aspirations, is a profound interference with a woman's body, and this is a violation of her security of the person.[6]

An Albertan, Joseph Borowski asked the high court to rule that abortions violated the fetus' right to life and equality. But is was decided that the fetus was not a person capable of claiming rights under the Charter. Eventually a legislative vacuum of sorts was created.

When Kim Campbell was Prime Minister, she tabled a bill to bring back a form of criminal law control over abortions. The item survived a close vote in the House of Commons on May 29, 1990 (140 to 131), but was defeated in the Senate by a rare tie vote (43 to 43) on January 31, 1991. There is now no Canadian criminal law which addresses abortion.[7]

So it is clear that God has been left out of the equation. The loud and well-funded pro-choice movements in both the U.S. and Canada have prevailed in their argument that having or not having children is a private matter for the pregnant woman to decide. "It's my body and I can do whatever I want with it."

The Scourge of Abortion

Physicians in the United States, 1.4 million times a year, disrupt and destroy the creative process of God with scalpels, saline and suction machines. It's called abortion. Let that number sink in.

One million, four hundred thousand children are killed each year.

It is estimated that more than 35 million babies have been butchered since *Roe v. Wade* in 1973.[8]

Recent debates have centered around "partial-birth" abortions. This barbaric procedure was pioneered by Dr. Martin Haskell. In this version of child-killing, the entire baby is delivered except for the head. (The doctors must make sure the head remains in the birth canal for the final act of brutality, or it would be classified legally as murder.) Then the baby's head is punctured with scissors and the brains are sucked out. There is ample evidence that the tiny child feels excruciating pain in his or her last moments.[9]

In April 1999, a baby was born after the first day of Dr. Haskell's multi-part, three-day, partial-birth abortion technique. The mother began to suffer abdominal pains and was rushed to Bethesda North Hospital in Cincinnati, Ohio. She gave birth to the twenty-two-week-old child that was supposed to have been aborted.

Nurse Shelly Lowe called the child "Baby Hope" because, she said, "I had hoped she would make it."[10] The nurse was not allowed to provide care—she could only comfort and rock the newborn. The emergency room physicians ruled that the baby's lungs were not developed enough to permit them to put her on a respirator. Baby Hope died shortly thereafter.

But many babies at twenty-two weeks can and have survived outside the womb. Gene Rudd of the Christian Medical and Dental Society said,

> The difference that apparently led doctors to let "Baby Hope" die is that she was the product of a failed partial-birth abortion. . . . This clearly crosses the line into infanticide—just like that practiced by the ancient Romans, who left their undesired babies out in the elements to die.[11]

Dr. Frank Joseph concurs: "It boggles my mind how a physician who has taken an oath to preserve life, can actually kill a defenseless unborn baby—literally ripped out, many times in pieces, from the mother's womb."[12]

The cause of causes is once again at work. Abortion is just another way of saying, "I will be like the Most High." This is original sin in one of its most despicable and insidious forms. God says, "Do not kill," and millions of Americans and Canadians respond with, "Oh really? Just watch me!" It is an attempt to circumvent the power of the Creator Himself. Rather than allowing God to decide the number of days in a human life, those who abort children cut that life off before he or she even has a chance.

Human Life Is Cheap, but Save the Whales

After the Columbine killings, Geraldo Rivera wondered aloud on his CNBC talk-show, "Where do these kids get the idea that life is cheap?"[13] Twenty-six years after *Roe vs. Wade,* we should all know the answer to that question, but no one really wants to talk about it because it might disrupt the billion-dollar abortion industry.

The right to abort an unborn child has undeniably communicated that life is cheap. How has this led to cold-blooded teenage killers? Follow my reasoning.

Respect for life is a basic principle. But when women are given the power to decide between life and death for that helpless baby in their wombs, that essential esteem is severely minimized. The child growing within becomes subject to the mother's whim and will. If she doesn't feel like having a baby right now, she can simply "terminate" it. It's not about the child, it's about the right to choose. And as soon as we place the right to choose over human life itself, we have cheapened that life immeasurably.

What is really the difference, then, if a mother kills the child before birth, five seconds after delivery or five years later? Shouldn't it still be the mother's choice? Most abortions are performed simply because the newborn would have been an "inconvenience" for someone. Why shouldn't parents be allowed to terminate the life of a two-year-old, a five-year-old or even a ten-year-old who has become an "inconvenience"? It's all about choice, isn't it?

As bizarre as some of this sounds, we have been on a slippery slope that is headed in this direction. And at the other end of the spectrum is another vulnerable class of people. Senior citizens may someday be considered "inconvenient" to our progress as a society. Skyrocketing medical costs could make it bothersome to keep the elderly around. Perhaps those with physical or mental handicaps will begin to "get in the way" too. It starts to look a lot like Hitler's Germany with its emphasis upon building a superior race. Why? Because all human life is no longer precious and valuable.

In stark contrast, many in our society are deeply concerned for the "rights" of animals and their humane treatment. For example, when an ancient Native American ritual that involved the killing of a young gray whale was nationally televised in May 1999, the outcry was incredible. Threats to kill Native Americans appeared on the Internet. Animal rights groups were outraged. The Associated Press reported:

> International officials are considering more humane ways of killing whales. Several environmentalist and animal activist groups argue that whales never should be killed because they are among the world's most intelligent creatures and feel mental anguish as well as physical pain.[14]

As I ponder this outpouring of sympathy over the anguish that a whale feels while being shot or harpooned, I am deeply troubled. This represents an obscene imbalance of priorities. A fully formed child can have his head "harpooned" in its mother's womb by a surgeon's scissors and most people don't even blink. But save the whales? That child was created in the image of God and has an eternal soul. There is no animal of any species that rises to the level of a human being in its intrinsic worth. And though I would never advocate wanton cruelty to animals, we need to get some perspective here.

Decades of decadence are beginning to catch up with the lawless, murderous mentality spawned by unfettered access to abortion. Writing to the Colorado legislature after the massacre in Littleton, Diane

Hocheaver and Leslie Hanks said, "For three decades, our youth have lived in a culture of death, been taught by the law that life, even the most innocent, is dispensable. Violence in the womb has begotten violence outside the womb."[15]

How could parents who agreed to an abortion tell their son not to get involved with a gang "because someone might get killed"? The boy could answer, "Don't tell me what to do—you just killed your baby!" One physician says:

> One would have to have the IQ of a turnip to think that the killing of 1.4 million unborn babies yearly does not give children the perception that life is cheap. Children are not stupid—they know what's going on in their own families and in their friends' families.[16]

There is a definite and disturbing connection between aborting "inconvenient tissue" and assassinating "annoying classmates and teachers." It's all about removing obstacles so that you can be in control of the situation. That is exactly what happened in Littleton, Colorado on April 20, 1999. Eric Harris and Dylan Klebold stood in the place of God and decided who would live and who would die on that day. And even as you are reading this chapter, there are pregnant women en route to abortion clinics to make a similar statement about human life: It's cheap.

Dr. Laura Schlessinger, the "queen of talk radio," asks, "Where's the leap?":

> We want our kids not to think of killing as a solution to temporary problems, so we'll put up signs about people killing their unborn infants because it's inconvenient. You've got a Dr. Peter Singer now at Yale in the Ethics and Human Values department saying that for the first twenty-eight days [after a child's birth] you should be able to kill your newborn if it's unacceptable. And you want kids not to shoot each other in schools? What? Are you out of your mind? Is there something wrong with you? Do you think for kids that is a huge leap? Inconvenient unborn child . . . annoying desk mate—where's the leap? I'm in the middle of my prom . . . I have to drown my baby. Where's the leap?[17]

The Next Step Down: Stem Cell Research

> In a cramped laboratory at Boston Children's Hospital, Evan Snyder toils over petri dishes packed with cells that the pediatric neurologist hopes will one day help youngsters with brain disorders. The cells, harvested from the brain of an aborted fetus, are neural stem cells, the building blocks of the human brain.[18]

In November 1998, private researchers discovered how to isolate stem cells from the embryos and fetal tissue of unborn children. In June 1999, a presidential advisory panel recommended that federally funded researchers be permitted for the first time to conduct certain types of studies with the tissue of aborted children. Listen to their reasoning:

> The panel will recommend supporting embryo research only on spare human embryos donated by fertility clinics. "There is a consensus forming that it is permissible to conduct this type of research on embryos left over from [in vitro fertilization] procedures where they would have been discarded in any event," says Thomas Murray, chairman of the NBAC's [National Bioethics Advisory Commission] genetics advisory subcommittee. "Do you thaw and throw them away or use them as a source of stem cells?"[19]

Please take careful note of the words being used here: "cells . . . harvested from the brain"; "spare human embryos"; "embryos left over." Harold Shapiro, chair of the NBAC, points to the key question answered by God thousands of years ago: "When does biological material achieve the moral status of a person?"[20]

Judy Brown, president of the American Life League in Stafford, Virginia, answers the inquiry without flinching. "An embryo is an embryo at fertilization—period. What they're proposing is to take tiny babies, redefine them as scientific material and destroy them for the purpose of research and experimentation. And that's immoral."[21]

The scientific debate is cleverly disguised with the promise of helping youngsters with brain disorders as well as battling diabetes, Alzheimer's and Tay-Sachs diseases. But no amount of arguing the potential benefits can hide or erase the simple fact that these innocent human beings are being treated like lab rats—cut them, study them, use them, discard them.

Just how much longer will God allow this kind of barbaric "research" to continue? When will He pull the plug on these murderous acts? When will it be "game over"? Perhaps we are already seeing the beginning of the end in places like Littleton, Colorado.

Reaping What We've Sown

It was Leonard Ravenhill who once said, "If God doesn't judge North America soon, He will have to apologize to Sodom and Gomorrah." As we consider the murder and mayhem that is sweeping the country, Ravenhill's words ring true. But Jehovah's judgment does not always come as direct bolts of lightning. Fire and brimstone are not His only forms of retribution. Sometimes it is the simple fulfillment of a basic life principle: We reap what we sow.

> Don't be misled. Remember that you can't ignore God and get away with it. You will always reap what you sow! Those who live only to satisfy their

> own sinful desires will harvest the consequences of decay and death. But those who live to please the Spirit will harvest everlasting life from the Spirit. (Galatians 6:7-8)

Do the school yard massacres, in part, represent a bitter harvest from legalized abortion? Having sown the destruction of innocent unborn children, should we not reap the hellish fruit of kids killing kids? If you will allow it, this will begin to make perfect sense. We have planted seeds of abortion which said, "Life is cheap." We have watered those seeds with movies and music and games and Internet pages which glorified violence and murder. So now it's harvest time. Bullets are flying and bodies are falling in schools across the nation.

This is the abortion distortion. The dismembering of innocent unborn children has twisted our entire value system.

The human race cannot play with fire and not expect to get burned. God will defend the rights of the unborn child even if the laws of the land will not. In shooting after school shooting, I believe the Creator has been sending a strong message. God did not cause these events, but neither did He stop them. We made this bloody bed and we will now have to lie in it. The Creator is making us see the end result of our flippant devaluation of human life as evidenced in abortion.

A closing word in this chapter about those precious little souls who never made it to the outside of their mothers' wombs. They are—millions and millions of them—

> Safe in the arms of Jesus,
> Safe on His gentle breast,
> There, by his love o'er-shaded,
> Sweetly [their souls] shall rest.[22]

Though their existence was brief and painful, they now have their place of peace and joy everlasting in the kingdom of God. When we consider the torturous ways in which these priceless children were murdered, we can rest assured that they will never suffer again. "Unwanted" and "inconvenient" on this earth, these dear ones have been welcomed with open arms by their loving Creator. There, they will be cherished for all eternity.

The cause of causes can be found in sinful human nature. All the murder and mayhem starts here. We don't need to look any further than our own hearts to understand "why" anyone could kill another human being in a fit of rage. We were born with an evil nature which is prone to violence.

We can add to this the work of the enemy, Satan, who "prowls around like a roaring lion, looking for some victim to devour" (1 Peter 5:8). One of the devil's primary objectives is to bring about death—the death of both the human soul and body. This is his obsession. And Lucifer scored one of his largest victories ever in 1973 when the Supreme Court of the United States of America gave women the right to kill unborn children.

But there was a side benefit for Satan in the legalization of abortion. Human life itself was devalued for the generations that would follow. Certainly we have seen evidence of this guileful depreciation in school yard massacres from Pearl, Mississippi to Littleton, Colorado. Klebold, Harris and the other killers saw their victims as contemptible objects to be wasted.

The sin nature has had an influence in several other places too. Let's look next at its impact on parents.

Chapter 12

Parental Abdication

"Now the Bible is turned on its head: The sins of the sons are visited upon the fathers." [1]

—Ellen Goodman

Boston Globe columnist Ellen Goodman summarizes the intense national debate on parenting that followed the Columbine killings:

> In the days since the Littleton massacre, the country's eyes have turned to the families of Dylan Klebold and Eric Harris. We've racked up the evidence—a handwritten diary, a sawed-off shotgun on the dresser, bomb makings in the garage—and asked, "Where were the parents?"[2]

The writers, psychologists and other experts on this matter seemed neatly divided into two contrasting opinions in answering Goodman's simple question.

So where *were* the parents? Can we pin partial or secondary blame for this bloodshed on Wayne and Kathy Harris along with Thomas and Susan Klebold? Did they know anything at all about the violent tendencies or plans of Dylan and Eric? If so, how much did they know? And if so, when did they become aware of it? "Too late" isn't a good enough answer for the loved ones of the slain students and teacher.

Should the parents be held legally liable for these deaths because of the actions of their sons? Just what is the responsibility of parents when their children become mass murderers? These are questions that are being pondered by lawyers and mourning relatives in all of the places where kids have been killed by other kids.

The Law of the Land

Both Attorney General Janet Reno and Governor Bill Owens of Colorado have suggested that the parents of Eric Harris and Dylan Klebold might be held criminally responsible for their sons' actions. But legal experts say that such a case would be extremely difficult to prove. American law generally holds people accountable for crimes only when they actively participate, as in "aiding and abetting in a homicide."

Peter Arenella, a professor of criminal law at the University of California at Los Angeles, says the rush to blame parents is understandable. But he also indicates that there are several foundational principles in the American legal system that present serious obstacles to those seeking to vent their outrage through the courts. "One of those principles is that parents are not legally responsible for the criminal acts of their children unless they were aware they were going to commit such acts and failed to stop them."[3]

U.S. law generally requires prosecutors to prove that a defendant had the intent to participate in a crime in order to be found guilty. Although there is a special relationship between parents and their children, at present the courts have not said that mothers and fathers should be held criminally censurable for their children's acts simply because they are parents.

But others are looking for new ways to prosecute the legal guardians of children who commit such heinous assaults. President Clinton has announced a package of gun-control proposals, which includes a measure to hold parents answerable if their children commit crimes with guns. The county sheriff in Littleton, who found a sawed-off shotgun barrel and bomb-making materials in plain view in the bedroom of Eric Harris, said, "Parents should be held accountable for their kids' actions."[4]

There are many possible legal claims under both civil and criminal laws that could be lodged against the parents. Lawyers say that such suits in Colorado could seek unlimited civil damages by claiming that the parents of Dylan Klebold and Eric Harris were negligent in their supervision of the young men and "knew or should have known" about the stockpile of guns and bombs.

Half the states in the U.S. have enacted some form of parental responsibility law. Mothers and fathers can be held liable for moderate damages even if they did not know about the malicious acts of their offspring, such as vandalism. In some states, thousands of parents have been fined, required to attend counseling or even given a few days in jail for failing to properly supervise their delinquent kids.[5]

In Michigan a couple was fined for failing to supervise their drug-using, church-robbing, one-boy crime wave. A Florida mother was sentenced to probation because three of her five children refused to go to school. In Louisiana and California parents can go to jail if their kids join a gang.[6]

One particular Colorado law might become an issue in the Columbine murders. It is illegal for an adult to permit a juvenile to possess a firearm if the adult knows that there is a "substantial risk" that the youth will use it to commit a felony. If convicted, a parent would face two to six years in jail.

There is, however, a major sticking point in any such lawsuit, according to William Glaberson: "Because of the pervasiveness of guns in Colorado, the presence of the shotgun might not cause a reasonable parent to conclude that a crime was being planned."[7] Indeed, the evidence gathered in Littleton thus far gives no indication whatsoever that the Klebolds or the Harrises would have imagined that their sons posed a "substantial risk" of committing such atrocities.

Criminal defense lawyer Jeffrey Springer summed up the entire question in one short sentence: "Being an irresponsible parent who has blinders on is not a crime."[8]

Lots of Lawyers and Lawsuits

One month after the Littleton massacre, Michael and Vonda Shoels filed a $250 million wrongful-death suit against the parents of Eric Harris and Dylan Klebold. Their son Isaiah, eighteen, was the only African-American student slain in the Columbine rampage. The Shoels's attorney, Geoffrey Fieger, claimed that no rational person could believe that the teenagers "amassed an arsenal" without their parents' knowledge. "Justice demands a full accounting of everyone who significantly contributed to this massacre," Fieger argued. "Klebold and Harris could not have developed and executed their violence without the negligence of the parents and possibly others."[9]

Colorado law limits damages in a wrongful-death suit to $250,000 unless Fieger can prove that the parents knew of their sons plans and acted negligently. Thomas and Susan Klebold have been questioned by authorities, but Katherine and Wayne Harris have refused to talk until they are granted immunity. The

Harrises could, however, be compelled to testify in a civil case.[10]

This was the first in what is expected to be several suits targeting:

- School administrators
- Law-enforcement officials
- Gun manufacturers
- Movie production companies
- Music production companies
- Internet sites

The overwhelming grief and anger felt by the relatives of victims would make such lawsuits understandable. But legal experts admit that these would be difficult cases to win. Harvard law professor Alan Dershowitz says the blame should be placed solely on the shooters. "What we're talking about is an intentional, deliberate, criminal act. It would probably be illegal to hold parents responsible for their children's actions unless you can show some specific fault on the part of the parents."[11]

In defense of the Harrises and Klebolds, attorney Andrew Cohen of Denver, a legal analyst for the news media, said, "It may turn out that they knew their kids weren't angels. That's a very far stretch from proving [that they knew] the attack would take place."[12]

Sympathy for the Parents of Teenagers

Without offering absolution for the mothers and fathers of these teenage murderers, several writers have come to their defense for one simple reason: *We are talking about teenagers here!* As the father of two teenage daughters (sixteen and eighteen), I must say that I have a much deeper appreciation for all the parents who have gone before me. Before my children reached this stage, I had all the answers. Lately I've regressed to having all the questions.

"Kids lead secret lives," Joanne Sharpe is quoted as saying. "Sometimes it's impossible to know them. Sometimes they're way beyond your control."[13]

Sharpe speaks from experience. In September 1997, her eighteen-year-old son, Columbine senior Robert Craig, took a .22-caliber handgun from her bedroom. He killed his stepfather with a single shot to the head, then fatally fired the pistol through the roof of his own mouth.

But consider Robert's track record prior to this murder-suicide:

- He had a 3.8 grade point average.
- He had plans to attend college.
- He didn't drink or do drugs.
- He had a number of friends.
- He returned home before his curfew.
- He often told his mom he loved her.
- He had a close relationship with his stepfather.

Mrs. Sharpe said of her son, "I thought he was a pretty wonderful kid. Robert looked like every other kid at Columbine."[14]

She and her husband of eleven years had talked with Robert about college, safe sex, drinking and driving—all the things parents are urged to discuss with their kids. But she also ran into the frustrating wall of silence that every parent of teenagers eventually faces. "Have you tried to get a teenager to talk when they don't want to?"[15]

In a sarcastic tone, columnist Ellen Goodman pointed out how difficult it truly is to get into the mind of a teenager:

> At last the advocates of parental responsibility laws seem to have found their poster parents. . . . How reassuring it is to point a finger at Wayne and Kathy Harris, Thomas and Susan Klebold, as proof that we would have known—wouldn't we? How easy to cast them as "irresponsible" rather than listen to the minister who buried Dylan: "He was their son—but they don't know the kid who did this."[16]

There are secret places inside young hearts that are complex and contradictory. As parents, we so quickly forget our own experience—this volatile mixture of peer pressure, hormonal changes and parental expectations. Adolescence is most certainly a pressure-cooker, and mom and dad may not always be sure just how to interpret the steam. If I were to ask most adults the question, "What did your parents know of your inner life when you were seventeen?", the answer would most likely range from "not much" to "absolutely nothing."

One columnist concludes with this persuasive analysis: "Before we prosecute parents for the sins of their children, I have a question. Tell me what punishment the law can administer that's greater than a life sentence of pain for families who'll forever ask themselves 'Why?' "[17]

Defining Parental Responsibility

Though we may sympathize with the parents of teenagers who commit murder and mayhem, we must also squarely face one stubborn fact. In each case there was some level of parental abdication. "The cover of *Newsweek*'s May 10 issue shouts 'The Secret Life of Teens,' as if our children were aliens," observes columnist Syl Jones. "A far more important exposé worthy of our consideration would be, 'The Secret Life of Adults.' "[18]

The governor of Colorado, a father of three children, ages eight to sixteen, has been very outspoken in his views since the tragedy in Littleton. Writing the "Opposing View" for a *USA Today* editorial, he said,

> Where were the parents in this case? The evidence does not yet fully explain how their children

> could have conceived and executed a plot of this magnitude. Yet what we do know suggests an astonishing lack of involvement in the lives of two troubled young men. . . . They even made a video acting out their killing spree for a class project. It is both a duty and a responsibility of parents to be involved enough with their children to notice signs such as these. . . . Letting adolescent boys spend hours on the Internet without knowing what sites they visit, whom they chat with, and what is on their personal home page is an abdication of parental responsibility.[19]

Writing in *Time*, Amy Dickinson asks some troubling questions:

> Is it possible for parents to miss homicidal rage? I can't help asking: Where were the Harrises and Klebolds when their sons were watching *Natural Born Killers* over and over? Have the parents seen that movie? Have they ever played *Doom* and the other blood-soaked computer games that occupied their children? . . . Were the Harrises aware of the pipe bomb factory that was in their two-car garage? The kid down the street was aware of it, and he's 10 years old.[20]

Charles E. Greenwalt II catalogues another aspect of parental abdication:

> Every week, the average American child between the ages of 2 and 11 watches 1,197 minutes of TV and spends 39 minutes talking with his parents. Fifty-two percent of kids between 5 and 17 have a TV in their bedroom. Every year, the average teenager spends 900 hours in school and 1,500 hours watching TV.[21]

Greenwalt continues with more grim statistics:

- During prime-time viewing hours on any given evening, at least fifty people are shot, killed, maimed or raped on programs on broadcast and cable TV channels.
- Eighty percent of television producers believe there is a link between TV violence and real-life violence.
- Fifty-four percent of local TV newscasts are devoted to stories about crimes, disasters and wars.

And this is just the influence of TV. Add to this the sewer of sex and violence coming from music, videos, computer games and the Internet. The columnist concludes, "American society has been sitting on a bomb, and it has exploded."[22]

There is no way parents of this generation can escape these glaring realities. We are responsible for the things our children see and hear while they live in our homes. We are accountable for their use of time. We simply must admit that on too many occasions it has just been easier to allow the various media to become a baby-sitter. This is parental abdication defined practically in ways that should speak to us all.

We've Left It to Beaver

In many cases, baby boomers have rejected the counsel of past generations in regard to parenting. *Mom and Dad were much too harsh. We'll show them how it's done.* And so our approach has been to "leave it to Beaver." We've been more interested in being "friends" to our children than authority figures.

I know this temptation firsthand. My wife and I both came from homes with strict—but loving—parents. Relatively speaking, my daughters would consider me a strict father, but I have tried to be a little less "in your face" than my own mom and dad were. There are times, however, when I realize that Bill and Madonna Allen had a much better handle on this than I have.

No parent wants to be the bad guy; it's much easier just to go with the flow. But this is just another example of parental abdication. We have been placed on this earth to love, guide, discipline and reward our children—and not always in that order. Proverbs 22:15 is true for every generation: "A youngster's heart is filled with foolishness, but discipline will drive it away."

Discipline can be accomplished without harsh, degrading language or extreme brute force—but it must be done. And parents are the ones who have been commissioned to do it. The apostle Paul had this balanced style of parenting in mind when he wrote to fathers, "Don't make your children angry by the way you treat them. Rather, bring them up with the discipline and instruction approved by the Lord" (Ephesians 6:4). I'll have much more to say about this in chapter 20.

Peter Schmit, a social studies teacher at Wayzata High School in Plymouth, Minnesota, says that kids have not really changed all that much from the stereotypical Wallys and Beavers from the "Leave it to Beaver" TV show of the 1950s.

> It's the way that we, as adults, are responding that's changed, and to the detriment of the kids, in my opinion. As a parent, I have to go back to a 1950s mentality: "Here's the rule. If you break it, you're going to get nailed." That's the job of a parent.[23]

A Minneapolis columnist adds her "Amen" with these words of challenge to her fellow perpetually permissive boomers:

> Like it or not, we need to look at how our parents raised us, what it was about Ward and June that kept Wally and the Beav in line. We can't replicate the past, but many of its lessons stand the test of

> time better than we've wanted to admit. . . . We have waffled long enough about being authority figures. It was fun while it lasted, but it's past time for us to grow up.[24]

Parental Abdication and Kids Who Kill

Parental abdication was not the ultimate cause behind the mass murders at Columbine High School or anywhere else. Sin in the hearts of the shooters was the primary cause. These were stone-cold acts of deliberate, premeditated murder.

But the neglect and preoccupation of parents most definitely plays a part in the youth violence that is sweeping our nation. Our permissiveness has opened the door of opportunity for many evil influences that should have been shut out. When children feel they can break the laws of Mom and Dad with impunity, they begin to believe they can break the laws of the land as well without consequences. Parents become "aiders and abettors" of the sinful nature that is already present and active within their children.

And I submit to the reader that this temptation to be a wimpy parent is also part and parcel of our fallen nature. We have a natural bent to "look the other way." Confrontation is never easy. Setting limits is a very unpopular aspect of parenthood, but we must remember who originally wanted to remove all limitations. It was that snake in the Garden of Eden. Satan told Eve how foolish she and Adam were to allow the

Creator to set boundaries on their behavior. And we know how *that* turned out.

Sin, Satan, abortion, abdication—the picture is becoming more and more clear. We are getting to the confluence of factors that compose a sensible "Why?" By opening with the correct, biblical starting point, we will be able to get to the right finish line.

Next, we must take a careful look at virtual and visual violence.

Chapter 13

Virtual and Visual Violence

"Get in touch with your gun-toting, testosterone-pumping, cold-blooded murdering side." [1]

—Ad for a Sony video game

Violence is a tragic trait of fallen human nature. Brutality showed up early and often from the very beginning of creation. The first boy born to the first parents of the human race slaughtered his little brother in a rage of jealousy and anger. No TV or video game could be blamed there. Cain did not have "antisocial personality disorder." He was simply acting on his instincts as a sinful human being—"I am jealous, therefore I kill."

In testimony before the U.S. House Subcommittee on Crime, Darrell Scott, father of one of the victims in Littleton, said,

> The first recorded act of violence was when Cain slew his brother Abel out in the field. The villain was not the club he used. Neither was it the NCA, the National Club Association. The true killer was Cain and the reason for the murder could only be found in Cain's heart.[2]

By the time of Noah, the spirit of murder and mayhem had inundated our race: "Now the earth had become corrupt in God's sight, and it was filled with violence. God observed all this corruption in the world, and he saw violence and depravity everywhere" (Genesis 6:11-12).

The Apostle Paul listed "hostility, quarreling . . . outbursts of anger" as characteristics of the sinful nature in Galatians 5:20. James wrote about the "whole army of evil desires" within the human heart which can lead to "scheming" and "killing" to get what we want, when we want it (James 4:1-2).

The Loudness of the Lambs

This penchant toward savagery is evidenced in our morbid fascination with death and destruction. Movies like *Silence of the Lambs* testify to our blood lust. This film made more than $130 million at the box office. It's main character, played by Anthony Hopkins, was Hannibal "The Cannibal" Lecter. Hannibal told an investigator, "A census taker once tried to test me. I ate his liver with some fava beans and a nice Chianti."[3]

Entertainment Weekly said that as a result of Hopkins' portrayal "a pop-cultural bogeyman to end all pop-cultural bogeymen had been born."[4] This film won Oscars for best picture, director, actor, actress and screenplay—one of only three movies to sweep all five categories.

Silence of the Lambs creator Thomas Harris has just finished a follow-up book, *Hannibal.* In an eery twist of fate, this news broke onto the cover page of *Entertainment Weekly* just one week after the carnage at Columbine. Deirdre Donahue offered this critical assessment in her book review for *USA Today*:

> As people reflect on the shootings at Columbine High School, the gruesome Hannibal—predicted to be this summer's must read—raises disturbing questions about our national addiction to grisly, violent entertainment. . . . Fantasy violence doesn't seem so entertaining after seeing teenagers run screaming from high school. It seems sick to sit in the cozy comfort of one's living room and read for fun and pleasure about the squeals human beings make when their ears are cut off. . . . Book selling is in a sick, sad place when Hannibal is this summer's must read.[5]

The character of Hannibal showed up first in Harris' book *Red Dragon.* Producer Dino De Laurentiis turned that story into the 1986 movie *Manhunter.*

Scottish actor Brian Cox was the first man to play Lecter. His comments are important here: "I was interested in that kind of childlike immorality that Lecter had. And while a lot of people get off on him, I never imagined him as the heroic figure he became. I still have a problem with that."[6]

This is "The Loudness of the Lambs." Something very noisy and frightening is being said about a society that reveres and celebrates a character like Hannibal Lecter. Our inclination for bedlam and gore gives incredible insight into the nature of man.

Consider some other everyday illustrations:

- When passing the scene of a car accident, we find it impossible not to look at the twisted wreckage. The presence of an ambulance makes it even more intriguing. I was hit by a car when I was an eleven-year-old boy. Just before I lost consciousness, I will never forget the huge crowd that had gathered to stare at me as I lay motionless on the pavement.
- Many of our most popular sporting events involve violence—football, boxing and hockey, to name just a few.
- News reports highlight murder and mayhem because they know that this will attract viewers and listeners.
- The tainted fascination with tragedy even shows up in the massacre at Columbine High School. A survey by the Pew Charitable Trust found that the Littleton shooting is "one of the

most closely followed stories of the decade."[7] The news media was criticized for the way in which they relentlessly covered this story, but they were doing it for one reason: They knew we would be watching!

Sex Sells—and Violence Too

Sex isn't the only thing that sells. Murder and mayhem also have a huge market in our society. Business people refer to it simply as "the law of supply and demand." We have demanded it by spending our dollars to view and listen to savage scenes and sounds. As a result, TV networks, movie producers, video game manufacturers, record companies and book publishers supply even more of it. "The violent-entertainment complex survives," Steven Levy of *Newsweek* argues, "because it caters to us: its brutal images and dark-side pursuits exist because they're popular and profitable."[8]

Thanks to their appeal to our culture's aberrant addiction to violence, many companies have been laughing all the way to the bank. "The success of this effort can be seen in the stock market," Charles E. Greenwalt II notes. "Time Warner, CBS, GE, Fox, Sony, Interscope, and yes, even Disney, have all seen their shares skyrocket in value. Investors who have profited from this bonanza may include residents of Littleton."[9]

Sadly, some in the film industry are even suggesting that the school massacres may actually serve to promote violent films. At the 1999 MTV Movie Awards, filmmaker Bobby Farrelly made a bizarre and cynical attempt at dark humor when he said that he hoped "someone will think of us" after the next school shooting. He was envious of the attention drawn to violence-laden films like *Natural Born Killers*, *Pulp Fiction*, *The Basketball Diaries* and *The Matrix*.[10] MTV executives wisely decided to delete those cruel comments before the awards show aired.

An important reminder is crucial here: Those in the entertainment industry did not create this violence in the human heart. No one had to. Cruelty is in each of us from the day of our birth. The various media can only serve to stir up that which is already within us.

It comes as no big surprise, then, that wicked people would seize the opportunity to profit in every way from this prurient attraction to annihilation. One of the goals of this book is to demonstrate how the sinful inclinations in every human heart play a role in the decisions we make every moment of every day.

What would drive a person to create a "game" where the primary objective is to murder or maim the people on the screen in front of you? There can be only one answer: a fallen nature. Only a wicked heart would devise ways to make money by exploiting the inclination to anger and revenge in others. This is at the center of the greed that drives pornographers, pimps, drug dealers and all the other vice-mongers in our world. One word describes both the dealer and the buyer: sinner.

Games of Death

The *New York Times* gives us an introduction to the bloody video games that have been at the center of the controversy surrounding the school shootings between 1997-1999:

> Games like *Doom* and *Doom II* and *Quake* are relentlessly first-person. The screen portrays the player's field of view, and the only visual token of the player's identity is the gun barrel that protrudes into the bottom of the frame. In most of these games, the setting and the violence are inherently unrealistic. What is realistic, in a nightmarish way, is the sense of rushed three-dimensional movement and the shift in skill levels that occurs as a child plays more and more. After a few hours of *Doom*, a child isn't virtually more skillful at pointing and shooting, he is actually more skillful. As a player improves, he is rewarded by an increase in the level of violence.[11]

John Leo, columnist for *U.S. News & World Report*, asks one of the more chilling questions in regard to the shootings in Littleton, Colorado:

> Was it real life or an acted-out video game? Marching through a large building using various bombs and guns to pick off victims is a conventional video-game scenario. In the Colorado massacre, Dylan Klebold and Eric Harris used pistol-grip shotguns, as in some video-arcade games. The pools of blood, screams of agony, and pleas for mercy must have been familiar—they are featured in some of the newer and more realistic kill-for-kicks games. . . . And they ended their spree by shooting themselves in the head, the final act in the game *Postal*, and, in fact, the only way to end it.[12]

Psychologist David Grossman of Arkansas State University is a retired Army officer. He coined the term *killology*—the study of the methods and psychological effects of training army recruits to be able to kill fellow human beings. Grossman points out the purpose behind the desensitization that takes place at boot camp:

> This brutalization is designed to break down your existing mores and norms and to accept a new set of values that embrace destruction, violence, and death as a way of life. In the end, you are desensitized to violence and accept it as a normal and essential survival skill in your brutal new world.[13]

Shooting the enemy becomes the result of a "stimulus-response" pattern that is repeated over and over. In World War II, infantry training used bull's-eye targets. But soldiers today learn to fire at realistic, man-shaped silhouettes that pop into their field of view. This has substantially raised the killing rate on the modern battlefield.

Dr. Grossman proceeds to point out the inherent danger in point-and-shoot video games. Children are learning the exact same conditioned reflex and motor skills that have proven to be so effective for the military. Michael Carneal, the schoolboy shooter in Paducah, Kentucky, is a prime example of this. He fired twenty-one shots, hitting nineteen students either in the chest or the head. ("Head shots" pay a bonus in many video games.) How could he be so accurate? By his own admission, Carneal had 3,000 hours of practice with point-and-shoot video games![14]

Andrew Golden, eleven, and Mitchell Johnson, thirteen, fired twenty-seven shots in the Jonesboro, Arkansas school massacre. They hit fifteen people from a range of over 100 yards. "That's pretty remarkable shooting," Grossman says. "We run into these situations often—kids who have never picked up a gun in their lives pick up a real gun and are incredibly accurate. Why? Video games."[15]

Today's video games have more realistic touches, which help blur the boundary between fantasy and reality: guns that are carefully modeled after the real thing; accurate-looking wounds; sound effects like screams and the recoiling of a heavy rifle.

U.S. News & World Report observes:

> Some newer games seem intent on erasing children's empathy and concern for others. Once the intended victims of video slaughter were mostly gangsters or aliens. Now some games invite players to blow away ordinary people who have done nothing wrong—pedestrians, marching bands, an elderly woman with a walker. In these games, the shooter is not a hero, just a violent sociopath.[16]

In "The Gaming of Violence," the *New York Times* discusses the inherent danger in the promotion of a self-absorbed reverie of rage.

> The fantasy embodied in video games is a narcissistic fantasy of rage. The psychology it profiles is brutally simple: an armed first-person actor in a hostile world full of completely dehumanized targets. This is a fantasy that inevitably prevents the player from personifying his assailants, which is why it has worked so well as a form of military training. The danger lies in the way video games channel and limit imagination as well as in their apparent violence.[17]

Appearing on MSNBC, David Grossman described an alarming new version of the game *Duke Nukem III*. This one enables the player to scan photos of real people (such as those in a school yearbook) and "morph" them onto the figures in the game. Then the shooter can kill enemies with a more personal touch.[18] The implications of this in the light of recent schoolhouse slaughters is deeply disturbing.

And yet some people still defend modern video games for "normal" youngsters. "There is no evidence that exposure to violent video games by well-adjusted young people causes them to have violent behavior," technology lecturer and author Don Tapscott claims. "Games are more lifelike today, but that does not mean that the people who play them confuse fantasy and reality."[19]

But this is one of the troubling traits of every school shooter described in the earlier chapters of this book—they had every appearance of being "normal" and "well-adjusted." Mr. Tapscott wants us to believe that these boys were demented or demon possessed. However, there is simply no proof of mental illness or any other deformity that could have triggered these massacres.

These blood-and-guts video games *did* have a treacherous impact on sane children from decent homes. I agree that the games in themselves did not "cause" the violent behavior. But they did provide graphic stimulus for boys who, like all of us, were born with a fallen nature. When mixed with that sinful nature's inclination to kill, this technology became a lethal tutorial on how to hit human targets.

Another factor to consider is that even though not everyone who plays violent video games becomes a mass murderer, everyone who plays is affected. The desensitization shows up in other ways and in other relationships. Dr. Grossman compares it to cigarette smoking: “Not everybody who smokes gets cancer. But they will all get sickened.”[20] Jeanne Funk, an associate professor of psychology at the University of Toledo, points to a recent study of sixth-grade video game players, in which many seemed to be desensitized to violence in general. “We found signs that children who enjoy these games can lose the emotional cues that trigger empathy.”[21]

Any attempt to refer to these video games as “harmless over-the-top jokes” is ridiculous, argues John Leo. “The bottom line is that the young people are being invited to enjoy the killing of vulnerable people picked at random. This looks like the final course to eliminate any lingering resistance to killing.”[22]

“We have to start worrying about what we are putting into the minds of our young,” warns David Grossman. “Pilots train on flight simulators, drivers on driving simulators, and now we have our children on murder simulators.”[23]

Littleton’s lessons are being learned close to home. Legislators are working to remove five video games that involve extreme violence and killing in the arcade at Denver International Airport. Representative Scott McInnis, R-Colorado, wrote to Denver Mayor Wellington Webb to request their immediate removal, and Webb agreed.[24]

Terror on Television, Mayhem at the Movies

Once again the President of the United States is commissioning a comprehensive study of the effects of media violence on American youngsters. I say "once again" because similar studies were commissioned in 1972 and 1982, and we already know what the conclusion will be. The *New York Times* reports: "Hundreds of studies done at the nation's top universities in the past three decades have reached the same conclusion: that there is at least some demonstrable link between watching violent acts in movies or TV shows and acting aggressively."[25]

In fact, "The evidence is overwhelming," says Jeffrey McIntyre, legislative and federal affairs officer for the American Psychological Association. "To argue against it is like arguing against gravity."[26]

The data suggests that the results are cumulative rather than catastrophic. In other words, viewing unrestrained violence does not immediately result in someone acting more aggressively than they might have moments before. Instead it is a progressive, sometimes insidiously passive change that takes place. Researcher Rowell Huesmann of the University of Michigan told a Senate hearing, ". . . just as every cigarette increases the chance that someday you will get lung cancer, every exposure to violence increases the chances that someday a child will behave more violently than they otherwise would."[27]

In poll after poll, the public agrees with this correlation between visual and actual violence:

- In 1954, seventy percent of respondents in a Gallup Poll felt that comic books, TV and radio could be blamed for teen crime.
- In 1977, seventy percent said there was a relationship between violence on television and the rising U.S. crime rate.
- In a poll conducted by *USA Today* (April 30-May 2, 1999), seventy-three percent said TV and movies share at least a little of the blame for teen crimes.[28]

One of the intrinsic dilemmas in dealing with all of this is the normalization of murder and mayhem. We have become so saturated in savagery that we can casually minimize its impact. Judy Gerstel, film critic for the *Toronto Star*, frankly admits, "My own tolerance for [on-screen] violence may have become much greater. I've become inured to it."[29]

There was a time when violence on TV and in the movies was sanitized. Generations of boys grew up on the exploits of Roy Rogers, Gene Autry and other matinee idol cowboys. Their blazing six-shooters rarely missed the bad guys but, curiously, never drew blood. The criminals just fell down dead without so much as a bullet hole in their shiny black vests. This sterilized style of shooting was due in part to the Motion Picture Production Code (MPPC).[30] The idea was to entertain audiences, not upset them.

In 1953 the MPPC took a major hit in the film *Shane*. The death of the farmer at the hands of a professional killer was intended to shock. The victim was lifted off his feet by the velocity of the bullet and flung backward. He went sliding down a muddy street as if shot from a cannon. Audiences had never seen anything like it. According to Robert W. Butler, the film seemed to say, "This . . . is what violence is really like. It's ugly and ignominious, not neat and tidy like you've been led to believe."[31]

Then in the late '50s and '60s, the MPPC eroded rapidly. The one movie that rewrote the book on film violence was the 1967 flick *Bonnie and Clyde*. A romanticization of real-life 1930s bank robbers Bonnie Parker and Clyde Barrow, it filled the big screen with blood galore, gaping wounds and bullets too numerous to count.

One year later director Sam Peckinpah raised the ante with his film, *The Wild Bunch*. This was famous for its "blood ballets"—brilliantly staged slow motion footage of men being struck by several rounds of ammunition. One critic offered this assessment:

> Peckinpah claimed he wanted to show the horror of violence, but in retrospect one wonders if he didn't make it seem almost too dream-like, too beautiful. In fact, with its armies of extras going down in graceful arcs of splattering gore, *The Wild*

> *Bunch* opened the door to what might be called "high body count" violence.[32]

The carnage continued in 1977's *Star Wars*. By encasing the bad guys—imperial storm troopers—in helmets that masked their features, director George Lucas allowed the good guys to slay them with impunity. Storm troopers thus became dehumanized. They could have just as easily been moving targets in an arcade game.

Movies in the '80s combined this "faceless enemy" approach of *Star Wars* with graphically enhanced special effects. In film after film Arnold Schwarzenegger, Sylvester Stallone and Bruce Willis mercilessly mowed down entire armies of villains. The bullet-riddled losers could have been Vietnamese soldiers, drug gangs, gun-happy criminals—virtually any opponent who could be deemed worthy of audience contempt. They were less than human, and therefore didn't "count" when they were blown away.

"Not only were viewers invited to admire the creative ways in which these nonhumans could be dispatched (bullets, explosions, stabbings, high-speed crashes)," Robert W. Butler says, "we were encouraged to applaud them, to laugh at the look of surprise on a drug gunman's face when he discovers our hero has the drop on him."[33]

In more recent times, the new and the most disturbing genre of fury flicks has appeared. Consider a few illustrations summarized by *Time* over the past ten years. These could easily be woven together as a game plan for Littleton:

- *Heathers* (1989): A charming sociopath engineers the death of jocks and princesses.
- *Natural Born Killers* (1994): Two kids cut a carnage swath through the Southwest as the media ferociously trail them.
- *The Basketball Diaries* (1995): Druggy high schooler Leonardo DiCaprio daydreams of strutting into his homeroom, donning a long black coat and gunning down a hated prof and half the students.
- *The Rage: Carrie 2* (1999): Jocks viciously taunt outsiders until one girl commits suicide and another wreaks righteous revenge. Carrie uses her telekinetic powers to pulverize a couple dozen kids.
- *The Matrix* (1999): Keanu Reeves stars in a black trenchcoat lined with enough firepower to end World War III. It's a tale of outsiders against the Internet druids.[34]

Denver Archbishop Charles Chaput oversees the Roman Catholic archdiocese that includes Columbine High School. Since the killings, Chaput went to see *The Matrix*. While watching the film's slow-motion killing scene, he said, "It occurred to me that Mr. Harris and Mr. Klebold may have seen that film. If they did, it certainly didn't deter them."[35]

A columnist for *U.S. News & World Report* said that in *The Matrix*, "Keanu Reeves's slaughter of his enemies is filmed as a beautiful ballet. . . . The whole scene makes gunning people down seem like a wonderfully satisfying hobby, as if a brilliant ad agency had just landed the violence account."[36]

Does any of this sound familiar? These murderous movies persuade us to view unrelenting violence as dark comedy. The goal seems to be to get audiences to laugh at and applaud that which should have saddened and appalled us. One writer summarized the terrifying way in which these daydreams of happy destruction became nightmares of hellish reality on April 20, 1999:

> It's easy to shrug all this off as little more than voyeuristic fantasy—until one considers the image of Eric Harris and Dylan Klebold moving deliberately through Columbine High, randomly shooting their fellow students. It is, of course, a scene that could have come from a high-body-count movie. To the shooters the victims weren't human—they were "jocks" or "heathers." Shoot one, make a wisecrack, laugh and move on to the next sucker.[37]

So the question is: Does screen violence so desensitize us that it paves the way for horrible events such as those that transpired in Littleton, Colorado? The answer is an unambiguous "Yes!" A *Kansas City Star* reporter challenges our twentieth-century claim to moral superiority over the ancient Romans, who made men and beasts fight to the death and called it "entertainment": "We've found our own way to enjoy that thrill: movie violence. And we think it's acceptable because nobody actually dies. Perhaps it's time to ask just what dies in us when we watch it."[38]

Defending the Indefensible

With reams of iron-clad proof regarding the definite connection between both visual and virtual murder and mayhem and the real thing, the entertainment industry is still trying to defend the rivers of blood flowing from both the small and large screen. Pointing the finger at violence in entertainment never works, according to Kristen Baldwin of *Entertainment Weekly*, and here's why:

> Because while graphic images can affect us—desensitize us, even—they do not, cannot create dangerous urges in people who don't already have those urges inside them. A well-adjusted kid who watches *Natural Born Killers* over and over—as Eric Harris and Dylan Klebold reportedly did—is not suddenly going to feel a need to commit a murderous act. Movies simply don't have that much power.[39]

Ms. Baldwin continues her argument by referring to all of the school shooters as "kids who are mentally disturbed," "antisocial," "nihilistic" and "unstable." It is only the deranged boys who can be affected negatively by nonstop carnage. No need to clean up the entertainment industry, which no doubt provides a nice living for Baldwin and her coworkers. Just find a way to isolate the sociopathic teens while the rest of us continue to wallow in gore galore.

This defense is incredibly weak and ludicrous. Here's a newsflash: Woodham, Carneal, Kinkel, Johnson, Golden, Klebold and Harris were not psychopaths. Reread chapters 3 through 7 if you must. They had sinful hearts full of jealousy, envy, pride, deceit and murder. With design, deliberation and plenty of help from the devil, they went on a killing spree much like what they had been witnessing for years on TV and in the movies. Is the media totally to blame? Of course not. But it was certainly a part of the witches' toxic brew.

To deny the media's liability by relegating these mass murders only to the work of the mentally disturbed is to miss a very important point: We are all "disturbed" from the day of birth. Adam and Eve were the defective parents of every human being. For this reason, unremitting violence will powerfully and negatively affect each person who is exposed to it.

It is impossible to predict who might explode next—but not because we can't identify who the "unstable" ones might be. Our forecasting is limited because it could be anyone. We live in a race that is 100%

infected by the disease of sin. To pretend that there is a special class of humans who are impervious to an overdose of visual or virtual murder and mayhem is the ultimate arrogance.

Hypocrisy in High Places

For those who might have hoped that our leaders in Washington, D.C. would help us overcome our addiction to violence, disappointment reigns supreme. Hypocrisy is springing up everywhere.

Right before the Littleton shootings, Vice President Al Gore was telling everyone that he and Tipper just loved *The Matrix*. Maureen Dowd explained this for us:

> It's easy to understand how the Father of the Internet could be so taken with the imaginative hit movie that is a video game writ large, a balletic and epic ode to violence about rebel hackers and society misfits who fight back when evil computers take over the world and reduce humans to AA batteries.[40]

But alas, the Gores' taste in movies directly collided with a White House effort to denounce the movie and video-game "culture of violence." According to reviewers, *The Matrix* has attracted an obsessively devoted audience of young and computer-savvy males. Bullets are flying everywhere. Shell casings glimmer alluringly in slow motion. The action has a backdrop of gorgeous techno-sheen. This violence entails a terrible beauty, and the death seems merely virtual. "There are eerie echoes of the dark underground world of the teenage Columbine killers, who laughingly treated death as virtual entertainment: Keanu Reeves throws open his long black coat to reveal an arsenal of pistols and machine guns."[41]

At one late showing of *The Matrix* in Washington, D.C., the similarities were so striking to several members of the audience that people began spontaneously yelling, "Columbine!" They cheered as Mr. Reeves walked through a metal detector, coolly pulled out his guns and blew away a large number of cops.

Ms. Dowd concludes by saying, "It's fine to like *The Matrix*. But you should not be entertained and financed by the same culture that you demonize and trash."[42]

Andrea Sheldon, executive director of the Traditional Values Coalition, reports: "This administration is owned and operated, bought and paid for, by the Hollywood liberal establishment."[43]

There are numbers to back up her statement. Saban, the creator of *Power Rangers*, is the second-largest producer of children's television programming. It is also the second-largest soft-money contributor to the Democratic Party. The company and its executives gave $328,776 to the party in the 1997-98 election cycle, according to Federal Election Commission records. Time Warner, which produced the brutal movie *Natural Born Killers*, gave Democrats $211,000 in that same period.[44]

This hollow hand-wringing among our leaders is offensive in so many ways. The principle of "supply and demand" comes back to haunt us again. The entertainment industry's "supply" of money for political campaigns places certain "demands" on those politicians, who dare not get too radical in proposing solutions or they will bite the hand that feeds them.

Perhaps all is not lost. I appreciated the courage of Senators Joseph Lieberman, D-Connecticut, and John McCain, R-Arizona, when they wrote "Toward a Safer Media Culture" in the *New York Times*:

> The various entertainment industries should declare a cease-fire in the marketing of ultraviolent products to children. Evidence presented at a Senate Commerce Committee hearing indicates that several top companies are aiming adult-rated movies and video games with high dosages of murder and mayhem at young teenagers. This is unethical and unacceptable . . . a safer, saner culture is attainable—if we want it.[45]

Do We Really Want It?

Listening to the people who have created the visual and virtual violence makes me wonder if we truly want that "safer, saner culture." Doug Richardson wrote the scripts for the gun-laden, kill-happy movies *Die Hard II* and *Money Train*. His defense of Hollywood's right to produce whatever sells goes like this: "If I were to accept the premise that the media culture is responsible, then I would be surprised that the thousands of violent images we see don't inspire more acts of violence."[46]

His point seems to be that the sheer volume of carnage is proof of its essential harmlessness. We should be seeing more murder and mayhem if the entertainment industry was to blame. Unfortunately Mr. Richardson may see this come to pass. Littleton may have been just the beginning of sorrows.

The creators of the video game *Doom* aren't talking. But Bob Settles is speaking out. He works on similar games for Bungee Software, which makes the popular *Myth II* game. Settles openly disputes the notion that racking up virtual body counts is a prelude to real-life killing sprees. "Mostly people who play our games get a little relief—it allows them to let out anger. I'm less worried about *Myth II* in the hands of a troubled teenager than the danger of having a gun in the household."[47]

Newsweek's Steven Levy responds with incisive reasoning:

> But isn't it logical to assume that a kid on the edge, after spending days immersed in these killer simulations, might gain a comfort level with the

> experience? . . . it's not an either-or situation: guns are all too available to troubled kids steeped not just in video-games or slash movies, but the entire volatile stew that's, well, America.[48]

Even the media's response to Littleton is another troubling example of our love affair with death and destruction. *Newsweek* bluntly commented on our fascination with home-bred violence: "The killers may have been steeped in a crock pot of fantasy carnage, but now the nation is willingly marinating in its very real aftermath: a tissue-consuming orgy of victim interviews and 911 tapes."[49]

Katie Couric did a very tasteful, emotional interview with two bereaved victims on the *Today* show shortly after the Columbine High massacre. But NBC and its cable sisters reran that segment as often as an MTV video in rotation. The line between actual news and tear-jerking "entertainment" became very blurry.

ABC's *Nightline* quickly pulled together a "town meeting" where victims from the latest student slaughter in Jonesboro, Arkansas were recruited to give comfort and guidance to Littleton survivors. Perhaps it was an honest attempt to help, but did it have to take place in front of millions of onlookers, complete with commercial breaks? This seemed to be little more than an intense competition to win the ratings war for the tragedy *du jour*.

One writer aptly summarized our enchantment with the media darling of destruction:

> What we're left with is a vicious cycle where even the examination of a disaster reinforces the violence-obsessed culture that may have helped trigger it. How can you pull the threads of violence from a society when those strands are so deeply woven into our character? We're left with a bromide: make sure that your kids don't get in so deep that fantasies cross over to horrible, heartbreaking reality. It'll have to do because the culture isn't changing. We like it too much.[50]

In an article entitled, "This Is Progress?", writer Cal Thomas encapsulates what we've learned so far: "When you mix the volatile ingredients of corrupted culture, vulgar entertainment, and broken, loveless families, you get child killers."[51]

Indeed, virtual and visual violence must be included in the explosive blend that becomes the answer to the question of this book: Why do kids kill? We must also factor in the work of Satan, who literally wants to damn you and me to hell. Another ingredient that must be added to this nefarious stew is the killing of innocent unborn children, which sends the message that life is cheap. Self-centered parents also contribute to kids killing kids when they choose to ignore rather than become involved, to avoid controversy rather than confront it, to spare the rod and spoil the child.

But remember—the real problem begins at birth: "The human heart is most deceitful and desperately wicked. Who really knows how bad it is?" (Jeremiah 17:9). Note how crucial it is to begin with the reality of our inbred tendency to do wrong—what theologians call original sin. When we try to start with the notion that human beings are basically good, we have no answer for the continual struggle that each of us has on the inside—we hate, we lust, we envy, we're proud. And when those common traits shared by us all are taken to the extreme, they show up on TV in blood-red color after the next school yard shooting.

Why do kids kill? For the same reason that anyone else commits murder. They have simply responded with greater energy to the evil impulses that are within every human heart. Yours? Yes. Mine? Yes.

Chapter 14

Musical Mayhem

"I try to show people that everything is a lie—pick the lie you like best, and I hope mine is the best." [1]

—Marilyn Manson

In 1982, I published a book entitled *Rock 'n' Roll, the Bible, and the Mind.* At the time it was considered somewhat radical because very few Christian writers were willing to confront the secular music industry with its lustful, violence-laced lyrics. Chapter 5 was called "Rock: The Music of Violence, Hate, and Aggression." A few excerpts will suffice to demonstrate the relative "innocence" of the statements and lyrics from the late '70s and early '80s:

We are the only ones crying out
Full of anger, full of doubt
And we're breaking all the rules
Never choosing to be fools.[2]
—From "Breaking All the Rules" by Peter Frampton

"Anarchy is the only slight glimmer of hope."[3]
—Mick Jagger of The Rolling Stones

"I'm interested in anything about revolt, disorder, chaos, especially activity that has no meaning."[4]
—Jim Morrison of The Doors

"We are all outlaws in the eyes of America."[5]
—Jefferson Airplane

"Rebellion is the basis for our group. Some of the kids who listen to us are really deranged, but they look up to us as heroes because their parents hate us too much."[6]
—Alice Cooper

"Ours is a group with built-in hate."
—Pete Townsend of The Who

On December 3, 1979, The Who were scheduled to do a concert at Riverfront Stadium in Cincinnati, Ohio. When the doors were opened, the crowd began to rush the gates with such force that a stampede ensued. Eleven teenagers were crushed to death that night. Pete Townsend later made this comment after hearing about the dead teens: "We're not going to let a little thing like this stop us. . . . We had a tour to do. We're a rock 'n' roll band. You know we don't worry about eleven people dying."[7]

As repulsive as all of this still sounds, it is extremely tame by contemporary standards—or lack thereof. One of the characteristics of sin is that it is never static. It always seeks the next lower level. We can clearly see this rampant digression in the years since I wrote *Rock 'n' Roll, the Bible, and the Mind*. The lyrics have become increasingly more vile and venomous.

Evidence of this deeper plunge into perversion can be seen in the development of warning labels for music. In 1985 the Recording Industry Association of America joined with the National Parent-Teacher Association and the Parents' Music Resource Center to create stickers for tapes and compact discs which are now used voluntarily throughout the music industry. These one-inch labels read: "Parental Advisory: Explicit Content."[8]

Individual companies determine which releases get the stickers. They are generally applied for profanity or graphic references to sex, violence or drugs. Some groups offer both "clean" and "explicit" versions. If you have not visited a music store lately, you may find it an overwhelming and educational experience. The wide variety of violence-laced music is beyond comprehension.

The Customer Is Always Right

The music industry, just like other entertainment venues we've discussed, is built around one simple idea: give the customers what they want. Gene Veith examines the implications of that in the context of sinful human nature: "The commercialized culture will give its customers whatever they want, so as to take their money. The appeal is to their desires. And, original sin being what it is, some of the deepest and most lucrative desires are sinful."[9]

This has led us to the popular music of our day that scorns authority, lauds illicit sex and lifts up pleasure as the only good. But it has gone further than that. Kids can choose to wallow in overt evil. White suburban teenagers now sway to Gangsta rap, which glamorizes rape, drugs and cop-killing. Death metal spins dark fantasies of vampirism, sadistic sexual experiences and outright demon worship. Marilyn Manson offers "music" about kids murdering their parents.[10]

World magazine offers an opinion on the huge popularity of this gory garbage:

> The aesthetic appeal is that of transgression: the thrill of rebellion, the tang of evil. Most listeners are content to enjoy such degradations in the privacy of their imaginations. Even though they never act them out, the spiritual impact remains. A very few are not content with the vicarious experience of evil, but want to play it out in the real world.[11]

Perhaps the saddest note of all is that *adults* (to use the term loosely) are the ones who have supplied the demand for shock rock. It is understandable that young people would think that musical mayhem is "cool." They are immature. But that also implies that they are too young to come up with this themselves. The most subversive elements of the pop culture are written, produced and sold to children by immature adults. One writer complains, "Corporate executives and stockholders are cashing in on the corruption of children. Is this the sign of a healthy culture? Or are we becoming more like animals that eat their young?"[12]

Witless for the Defense

> Our records have stickers with a warning from
> Tipper:
> " 'Coz they're no good for kids, If we'd get her we'd
> strip her."[13]

That little piece of poetry is from the now infamous rock band KMFDM and their song entitled, "Sucks." This was one of the music groups Dylan Klebold and Eric Harris listened to prior to their deaths by suicide. KMFDM stands for the German words "Kein Mehrheit Fur Die Mitleid" (roughly translated: "no pity for the majority").

Founded in 1984 in Paris, France by Sascha Konietzko, a German painter, and Udo Sturm, a multi-media performer, the band released their first album, "What do you know, Deutschland?" in December 1986. They moved to Chicago in early 1991. They were industrial-rock pioneers, blending machine-generated dance beats with pop melodies and random dissonance. The group disbanded in January 1999.

In an official press release one day after the Columbine killings, the former members of KMFDM went to great lengths to distance themselves from any liability whatsoever: "We are sick and appalled . . . by what took place in Colorado yesterday."[14]

But peruse the following lyrics to a few of their songs:

> Into this void I will give my self control
> Inside this noise is a weak and godless soul.[15]
>
> We got the power
> Excessive force.[16]
>
> It's the end of this world
> Something must end
> Time is right for a change
> It is all in our hands.[17]
>
> Forged from steel
> Iron will
> S— for brains
> Born to kill
> Son of a gun
> Master of fate
> Bows to no god, kingdom, or state
> Watch out
> Son of a gun
> Superhero #1.[18]

If I had a shotgun,
I'd blow myself to hell.[19]

It is easy to see how lyrics like the ones above would have a powerful impact on teenage boys who felt that they were very much in the minority. "No sympathy for the majority"—perhaps that mantra was floating in their brains as they casually walked the hallways of Columbine High with their guns and bombs.

Ann Powers, writing for the *New York Times*, offers insight into the effects of such excessive music:

> Today's extreme rock music, like most popular culture, sends a swarm of mixed messages. Its makers can be calculatedly brutish, and often fail when they try for subtlety. After all, they are operating in exile from adulthood, expected to be immature. Yet even the rawest extreme music offers adolescents a symbolic language with which to express the confusion they already feel. Communicating the anguish of victims and outcasts in a voice of vengeance and aggression, it theatricalizes rage.[20]

Marilyn Manson is another name that has surfaced in the debate over causes for the Littleton shootings. Though the truth is that neither Harris nor Klebold cared much for Manson's music or style, his band is considered the American epitome of the dark side of rock music. "This tragedy was a product of ignorance, hatred and an access to guns," Manson declared in response to suggestions that his music might have a connection to Littleton. "I hope the media's irresponsible finger-pointing doesn't create more discrimination against kids who look different."[21]

But consider the words to some of Marilyn Manson's songs:

> But I know I want to disappear,
> I want to die young and sell my soul.[22]
>
> I went to god just to see
> And I was looking at me
> Saw Heaven and Hell were lies
> When I'm god everyone dies.[23]
>
> Let's just kill everyone
> And let your god sort it out.[24]

Manson's web site is absolutely inundated with vulgarities of every imaginable kind, along with some you could not have imagined. Manson wrote an article for *Rolling Stone* magazine entitled, "Columbine: Whose Fault Is It?" It was filled with blasphemy. Speaking of Jesus Christ, he said,

> A half-naked dead man hangs in most homes and around our necks, and we have just taken that for granted all of our lives. Is it a symbol of hope or hopelessness? The world's most famous murder-suicide was also the birth of the death icon—the blueprint for celebrity. Unfortunately, for all their

> inspiring morality, nowhere in the Gospels is intelligence praised as a virtue.[25]

In defense of his "art form," Manson said, "I'm a controversial artist, one who dares to have an opinion and bothers to create music and videos that challenge people's ideas in a world that is watered-down and hollow."[26]

It's amazing just how "hollow" those words sound. Manson is skillfully preying on the disillusioned youth in our culture. He has learned that his level of income is in direct proportion to his level of outrage. If you are into freak shows, he offers the best charade since the reign of KISS in the '80s. All this talk about artistry and challenging ideas is a front for selling more albums, T-shirts and other Manson memorabilia. His cynical remark quoted at the beginning of this chapter speaks volumes. Marilyn wants us to believe that his lie is "the best." And his lie is turning out to be a lucrative one.

Christian reggae singer Erik Sundin, a 1989 graduate of Columbine High School, was being interviewed during Gospel Music Week in Nashville, Tennessee when he heard the news of the rampage. His comments at that time serve as a powerful rebuttal to the shock-rockers who are pleading "not guilty":

> Any message you put behind something as powerful as music only multiplies its influence. People like Marilyn Manson believe themselves to be

> harmless. I don't think that he even believes what he's doing—it's just a big show.[27]

Garbage in, Garbage Out

In these last two chapters, we have looked at virtual and visual violence along with musical mayhem. Both sides—the producers and the consumers—are deluded.

Those who create and promote this vicious smut demand impunity for any impact resulting from their products. Television and movie producers think they should be free to show any level of carnage they choose, and society should not hold them accountable. Musicians want complete liberty to sing about suicide, cop-killing and other death-demented themes and insist that no one will be affected.

Those who purchase and absorb these malicious materials want to pretend that it has no lasting influence. When parents allow children to spend endless hours with barbaric, shoot-em-all video games, to view slasher movies with gallons of blood spilled and to listen to violent music by vile musicians over and over again, how can they think there will be no consequences for assimilating this gore?

It is true that only a small percentage of those who are exposed to this kind of carnage end up shooting students and teachers at school. But does that mean that the principle of "garbage in, garbage out" does not apply? Not at all! There are bound to be consequences and repercussions of one kind or another.

Perhaps those who feed on a steady diet of murder and mayhem in their movies and music will become more apathetic about those in need around them.

Perhaps boys who watch slasher movies where females are treated like cows at a slaughterhouse will become abusive to their girlfriends and later their wives.

Perhaps those who consume quantities of death-friendly music will be more prone to depression and may never know a real sense of happiness and fulfillment.

These are just a few illustrations to underscore the fact that no one walks away from this culture of carnage unscathed. Input becomes output. Garbage in, garbage out. It is an inescapable law of the human mind. This is why the Apostle Paul talks about the importance of a "renewed" mind and thinking about the right kinds of things:

> Don't copy the behavior and customs of this world, but let God transform you into a new person by changing the way you think. (Romans 12:2)

> His [God's] peace will guard your hearts and minds as you live in Christ Jesus. . . . Fix your thoughts on what is true and honorable and right. Think about things that are pure and lovely and admirable. Think about things that are excellent and worthy of praise. (Philippians 4:7-8)

Did the music of KMFDM and others cause Eric Harris and Dylan Klebold to murder twelve peers and a professor? No. Two sinners made a choice to go on a rampage, and thirteen innocent people are dead as a result.

But that's not the germane question to ask about musical mayhem. We should be inquiring along these lines: *Did the music of KMFDM and others add fuel to the fire of their fallen natures? Did this music aid and abet the two boys who committed manslaughter?*

The answer is undeniably: *Yes!* The lyrics of lost musicians reached and inspired the hearts of two lost teenagers.

Next, what about the Internet and kids who kill?

Chapter 15

http://www.pipebomb.com

"With one mouse 'click,' kids could be in a porn shop, a pedophile's living room, a casino, a gun shop, a neo-Nazi hall, and Lord only knows where else." [1]

—Thomas L. Friedman

America Online was the Internet provider that housed the warped web site of Eric Harris. He had several user names including "Rebdomine," "rebldomakr" and "RebDoomer"—a reference to the computer video game *Doom.*[2] His postings included:

- A personal profile, listing the author as Eric Harris and stating his hobbies as: "Professional doom and doom2 creator, meeting beautiful females, being cool." For a personal quotation, he offered: "Quit whining, it's just a flesh wound—Kill Em AALLL!!!"
- Instructions on how to build pipe bombs: "Shrapnel is very important if you want to kill

and injure a lot of people. Almost anything small and metal will work, from paper clips cut into pieces to two-inch nails."

- A drawing of a creature toting a shotgun and a knife while standing on a pile of skulls.
- Song lyrics: "What I don't say I don't do./ What I don't do I don't like./ What I don't like I waste."
- A drawing of a man shooting automatic pistols, a large monster with horns and a boy, eyes wide, pointing two guns. In big red letters under this drawing are these ominous words: "I hate you. Eric Harris owns every single one of you: the fireworks will be set in the four twenty one!! Doom will become reality!"[3]

These cyberspace sketches of gunmen, statements of hatred and prophecies of destruction were fulfilled on the twentieth day of the fourth month, 1999. A web page filled with savage imagery and intense threats became reality, just as he said. What looked like mere ranting and raving became very real and excessively ruinous.

A Monster in Our Midst

The murder and mayhem wrought upon Columbine High School in April 1999 have forced us all to take a closer look at an incredible monster in our midst. This beast is getting bigger and meaner every day. Though originally intended to be a gentle giant who would help connect our world by the exchange of information and ideas, it is now clear that its temperament and agenda have changed.

Welcome to cyberspace and the World Wide Web of trouble.

It no longer matters what neighborhood you live in. Locking or not locking the door is not the issue. With the Internet, trouble is just a fingertip away. With the click of a button, all manner of evil can be staring us in the face from a computer screen. Steven Levy of *Newsweek* says, "It's undeniable that cyberspace offers unlimited opportunity to network with otherwise unreachable creepy people."[4]

Mr. Levy is right on. Consider a few illustrations:

- Pedophiles troll the net in search of innocent children with whom to chat. Then, hopefully a meeting. Finally, a chance to sexually abuse those children.
- Pornographers post their pictures and videos and interactive sex games luring the lustful into credit card debt.
- Blood-soaked video games like *Doom* can be downloaded for free on the Internet.
- Hate groups spew forth their venomous verbiage for anyone who will take the time to read or listen.
- Recipes for building bombs can be accessed by children of all ages. With lots of information but no experience, many kids are maimed or

> killed during the experimentation process. The ones who can figure it out go into high schools and blow up things and people.

These are just a few illustrations of wickedness on the web. The contrast of the available good and evil is quite arresting, according to columnist Thomas Friedman:

> It can be an incredible knowledge tool and an incredible microphone for hate. It can be a place where grieving Columbine students can come together to comfort one another and a place where a student outcast can nurse his grievances, research his revenge and find encouragement from neo-Nazis.[5]

One parent from Greensboro, North Carolina told the *New York Times*:

> Twenty years ago when I was in school, you didn't have access to millions of people to mess with your head. What is on TV is sort of controlled. What is in the movie theaters is sort of controlled. The influences that you can be exposed to on the Internet are just a lot more widespread.[6]

And it is all just one mouse click away.

Big, Very Big

Just how big is the Internet among our youth? What is the size, scope and monitoring of Internet use? According to Jupiter Communications, a market research firm, about 10 million American teenagers use the Internet.[7] It is projected that by 2002, 20.9 million kids will be online.[8]

CNN conducted the following poll on April 27-29, 1999 with 409 teens between the ages of thirteen and seventeen (the sampling error was plus or minus five percent):

Have you ever used the Internet?
Yes 82%
No 18%

When you have been online, have you ever seen Web sites with information on:
Sex 44%
Hate groups 25%
Bombs 14%
Guns 12%

How much do your parents know about the Web sites you visit?
A lot 38%
A little 45%
Nothing 17%

Do your parents have rules about how to use the Internet?
Yes, and I always follow them 31%
Yes, but I don't always follow them 26%
Parents have no rules 43%

Have you ever played computer games?
Yes 81%
No 19%

Have you ever played violent computer games?
Yes, regularly 8%
Yes, just a few times 40%
No, never played 52%

Do your parents have rules about the games you play?
Yes, and I always follow them 24%
Yes, but I don't always follow them 18%
Parents have no rules 57%[9]

There are several startling things in this poll. First, the sheer enormity of teens who are plugged into cyberspace. Then we see that sixty-two percent of parents know "little" or "nothing" about the web sites being visited by their teenage sons and daughters. That was certainly true in the case of the parents of Dylan Klebold, Eric Harris and some of the other school yard shooters.

Perhaps the most troubling statistic here is the fact that forty-three percent of these kids said their parents had established "no rules" for Internet use and fifty-seven percent had "no rules" governing computer games they played. It comes as no surprise, then, that fully forty-eight percent had played violent games "regularly" or "just a few times."

The Ultimate Test of Character

A popular definition of character is "who you are when no one is looking." In the light of that statement, I think most would agree that the Internet has become the ultimate test of personal integrity. Thomas Friedman drives this point home in rather eloquent fashion: "Precisely because the Internet is such a neutral, free, open and unregulated technology it means that we are all connected, but no one is in charge. The Internet is democracy, but with no constitution."[10]

The World Wide Web empowers people in ways that are not possible with television or newspapers. These broadcast-type media always include a producer or editor to make decisions for the viewing or reading audience. These men and women literally decide what we will see and hear. The Internet changes this entirely by giving people unlimited choices and unlimited power to make them. This has enormous implications for all of us, especially our children. "The only filter is the one you bring in your own head or your own heart, and since kids often lack the judgment microchip, it is even more critical that parents and educators provide it," Friedman concludes.[11]

Most parents pay attention to their children's TV viewing or use of the telephone. But this monitoring is even more important when it comes to the Internet. Why? It is interactive technology with no editor. Friedman synopsized the issue this way:

> If we are all connected and no one is in charge in cyberspace, then cultivating citizens in the school-

> yard or the backyard becomes that much more important. The more the Internet makes us all broadcasters, all researchers, all consumers and, alas, all potential bomb makers, the more critical it is that our teachers, parents and communities are still making us all citizens.[12]

Forbidden Fruit within Everyone's Reach

Throughout this book, I have affirmed the biblical principle that every human being was born with a sinful nature. We have this tendency, like our distant parents, to reach for the forbidden fruit. Unfortunately, the World Wide Web has bushels of corrupt produce just waiting to be fondled and tasted. And this fruit is hanging where everyone can reach it. Even though there are thousands, perhaps millions of hours worth of wholesome, informative, creative and useful items on the Net, human nature will yearn to peek into the dark corners. And let's not pretend that adults do not struggle with this reality along with their children.

It should not shock us that teens are surfing the web for guns, bombs, pornography, neo-Nazi nonsense and other vile, violent images. The "taboo" label makes the debauchery far more attractive and appealing than it could ever be in reality. For this reason, Adam and Eve were extremely disappointed with that tree in the middle of the Garden of Eden. It failed to deliver what the serpent had promised. How could he lie like that?

The World Wide Web did not crawl up the phone lines at the homes of Eric Harris and Dylan Klebold and then force them to kill thirteen people in their high school. We know why they did it. It was a willful act that arose from the hatred and jealousy of their sinful natures.

Having said that, we cannot dismiss the powerful influence of the Internet in our culture today. A world of iniquity is available at the click of a mouse. Klebold and Harris gained nefarious information for their prolific bomb building on the Net. They were able to maintain a web site filled with dire warnings, hateful statements and morbid sketches. Through e-mail they were able to plan their atrocities.

Is the Internet too free? For that matter, what about the terrifying abuses of the "right to bear arms" and the "right to free speech" evidenced in Littleton and elsewhere?

Read on.

Chapter 16

The Wrong of Rights

"Shoot him—with a .44-caliber Bulldog." [1]

—Filmmaker Spike Lee,
referring to National Rifle Association
President Charlton Heston

OK, class, it's time for a little history lesson. Today's topic is "Amendments to the United States Constitution."

The first ten amendments were proposed by Congress on September 25, 1789. They became known as the Bill of Rights and took effect on December 15, 1791. This book must address the first two—the freedom of speech and the right to keep and bear arms. Here is the exact wording of the First and Second Amendments to the Constitution of the United States of America:

> Amendment 1: Congress shall make no law respecting an establishment of religion, or prohibiting the free exercise thereof; or abridging the

> freedom of speech, or of the press; or the right of the people peaceably to assemble, and to petition the Government for a redress of grievances.
>
> Amendment 2: A well regulated Militia being necessary to the security of a free State, the right of the people to keep and bear Arms, shall not be infringed.[2]

As you can tell by the opening quotation from the ever-eccentric movie director Spike Lee, those who make their living off the First Amendment have been at odds with those who make a living off the Second Amendment. The tragedy in Littleton, Colorado had everyone running for cover to defend their own causes. It hasn't been a pretty sight.

Recently talk show darling Rosie O'Donnell, exercising her free speech right, brought Tom Selleck onto her show, obstensibly to discuss his new movie, *The Love Letter*. Instead she ambushed Selleck for exercising his right to bear arms and his alliance with the National Rifle Association (NRA), even though he is no longer a spokesman for them. Then the NRA attacked Rosie because she does ads for K-Mart, the number-one gun retailer in the U.S. Then Rosie defended that choice by pointing out that K-Mart no longer sells handguns, just hunting guns. As I said, it hasn't been pretty.

Examining the Freedom of Speech

Speaking on NBC's *Meet the Press*, former education secretary William Bennett made this salient comment after the bloodbath at Columbine High School:

> If these kids were walking around that school in black trench coats saying "Heil Hitler," why didn't somebody pay attention? I guarantee you if little Cassie Bernall . . . and her friends had been walking through that school carrying Bibles and saying, "Hail the Prince of Peace, King of Kings," they would have been hauled into the principal's office.[3]

This is a point well made and it leads us into an important discussion about the meaning of that important phrase "freedom of speech." In the minds of the framers of the Constitution, it referred to the freedom of people to speak to their leaders and be heard. Unlike England, where the monarchy was able to command the loyal subjects, Americans would have a voice in government.

In its context, freedom of speech was one of several provisions to ensure that no individual or governing body could tell someone else how he or she had to think.

- It prohibited the establishment of one system of religious beliefs that would be binding on all.
- It allowed people to worship in their own way without government interference.

- It guaranteed that political columnists would be free to write their opinions about government leaders without fear of reprisal.
- It gave the people the right to peacefully protest in large groups and make their concerns known in this way.
- It enabled the people to petition the government for specific changes which they felt were necessary.

This was very different from the autocratic rule of the British colonies. Having come from that background, those who formed the Constitution were determined to set this nation apart from anyone's tyrannical rule.

If you haven't noticed, the interpretation of the phrase "freedom of speech" has changed dramatically from the intentions of our forefathers! Now it includes just about everything imaginable. Pornographers who peddle the lowest forms of smut claim that they are protected by the First Amendment. Striptease dancers and their nightclub owners hide behind it. Shock-jocks have used this right to fill the airways with unfiltered filth. The makers of ultraviolent video games and movies insist that their products are protected by the First Amendment.

The Case against Jenny Jones

This year a jury in Pontiac, Michigan fined the syndicated talk show *Jenny Jones* $25 million for negligence in the slaying of a gay guest who revealed his crush on a heterosexual man. Jonathan Schmitz became so enraged after learning that his secret admirer was another man that he shot and killed Scott Amedure three days after the show.[4] Roy Peter Clark, senior scholar at the Poynter Institute in St. Petersburg, Florida, points to this jury's damage award as a shift in America's love affair with the First Amendment:

> I think the First Amendment defends even stupid and irresponsible people, but a life-and-death case like this just invites these consequences . . . failure to exercise a reasonable amount of responsibility in the course of your business has consequences. I don't think Oprah (Winfrey) has anything to worry about, but Jerry Springer and Howard Stern are playing with fire.[5]

Robert Lichter of the Center for Media and Public Affairs, a Washington, D.C.-based research group, agrees. "Talk shows play on the public humiliation of emotionally vulnerable people, and these shows are going to have to be more careful about the layers they unpeel of people's psyches."[6]

Geoffrey Fieger, the lawyer for the slain Scott Amedure, said, "That type of human exploitation needs to be corralled. This is a renegade business."[7]

Renegade, indeed. Radio shock-jock Howard Stern has made a mockery of the freedom of speech. He went so far as to make crude, sadistic jokes about the killings in Colorado. His show is carried in Denver by

KXPK-FM. Here's what he said the day after twelve students and one teacher were murdered:

> There were some really good-looking girls running out with their hands over their heads. Did those kids [the killers] try to have sex with any of the good-looking girls? They didn't even do that? At least if you're going to kill yourself and kill all the kids, why wouldn't you have some sex?[8]

Could this possibly be what the framers of the Constitution had in mind when they wrote that "Congress shall make no law . . . abridging the freedom of speech"? Did they intend that this pathetic, forty-something adolescent could make light of such a hellish tragedy and bring further pain to those who were already swamped in agony? In response to these vulgar, grotesque comments, both Geico Direct Insurance and Snapple Beverages discontinued their advertising on Stern's program.

The First Amendment, Limited Edition

The notion of an unrestrained right to free speech is coming under careful scrutiny in the aftermath of Columbine. Senator Orrin Hatch, R-Utah, reminded the Senate of the outrage Americans felt when it was discovered that tobacco companies were marketing cigarettes to children. "We should be equally concerned," Hatch concluded, "if we find that violent music and video games are being marketed to children."[9]

Not surprisingly, Doug Lowenstein, president of the Interactive Digital Software Association, did not like Senator Hatch's comparison. His defense? "The difference between cigarettes and video games is that video games are constitutionally protected under the First Amendment."[10]

It is amazing to me how corporations will defend anything that threatens their bottom line. It took years for tobacco companies to admit that smoking causes cancer even though they had undeniable proof decades before. Then it took them several more years to confess that they were targeting children with their ads. Why all the fuss? Because billions of dollars are at stake.

Now the people who produce music, movies, television and video games are facing some of the same investigation. Are they actually within the boundaries of the First Amendment if their products are creating a climate which promotes murder and mayhem in our schools? (Please note that I did not say these things *cause* death and destruction; however, these forms of media most certainly share some of the blame.)

The various studios and computer companies must ask a simple question: "Are we a part of the problem or are we a part of the solution to the youth violence that has swept our nation?"

The right to free speech already has some limits. It is inappropriate—and illegal—to yell "Fire!" in a crowded theater; no one can make threats against your life while hiding behind the First Amendment; child pornography is not protected. There are boundaries. I believe it is time for lawmakers to come up with some common-sense regulations. Some lines need to be drawn in the sand. Our democracy will not crumble simply because we set reasonable limits to the kinds of things that can or should be seen and heard.

For example, should we allow video games to be produced which mimic the remorseless murdering of human beings? Is it free speech or just big profits?

Should we stand idly by while musicians glorify death, violence and suicide? Are they really artists enjoying the protection of the First Amendment, or are they just greedy rock stars cashing in on teenage angst?

Is there redeeming social value in films that celebrate murder and mayhem? Should Hollywood really be free to produce such vicious garbage so that we can boast about our lack of rules as a democratic society?

Sometimes our "rights" can be dead wrong. William Bennett has assailed the major media for what he calls their "predatory capitalism." Although he acknowledges that, technically speaking, the First Amendment gives great latitude for expression in the arts, he asks pointedly, "Do you have no sense of decency?"[11]

Some years ago, Cardinal Roger Mahony, Roman Catholic Archbishop of Los Angeles, made a speech that shocked Hollywood. The movie moguls thought he would be calling for a tough new film-rating code, and they were prepared to be offended. But instead of calling for that code, the cardinal issued a pastoral letter defending artistic freedom. He appealed to moviemakers to think more about how to handle screen violence. When mayhem is portrayed, he asked:

> Do we feel the pain and dehumanization it causes to the person on the receiving end, and to the person who engages in it? . . . Does the film cater to the aggressive and violent impulses that lie hidden in every human heart? Is there danger its viewers will be desensitized to the horror of violence by seeing it?[12]

If Oliver Stone had honestly answered these questions, *Natural Born Killers* might never have seen its first day on the set.

The Right of the People to Keep and Bear Arms

I would not be a good poster boy for the National Rifle Association. I have never had an interest in guns. I can remember my brother Tim and I messing around with a BB-gun. But when he accidentally (?) shot me in the rump one day, we decided it was too dangerous. Later, as a teenager, I was invited by my cousin Bobby to try out his high-powered rifle. I think he just wanted to see me fall to the ground as a result of the kickback. I did not disappoint him.

You have just read the complete tales of Tom Allen's experience with guns. Several years ago, my wife and I briefly discussed getting a pistol for protection after our home was vandalized, but we could not get over our fear of firearms. Suffice it to say that guns and my right to possess them have not been a big item on my agenda. I am the first to admit that I might feel differently about this matter if someone I loved had died of a gunshot wound.

The school massacres that have become all too common since 1997 have rekindled the debate over the Second Amendment. The last time things were this stirred up in the United States concerning gun control was in 1981 when President Ronald Reagan and his staff member, James Brady, were both shot by John Hinckley. At that time a number of laws were enacted to make it more difficult for criminals and mentally disturbed persons to purchase handguns.

However, despite the legislation that has been passed, those with enough determination to get guns can somehow find a way. Consider some of the tragedies we've already looked at:

- Andrew Golden stole guns from his grandfather for his killing spree in Jonesboro, Arkansas.
- Kip Kinkel used firearms that his father had given him to shoot his mother and father to death before his rampage in Springfield, Oregon.
- Dylan Klebold had his girlfriend buy three guns because he was underage. A twenty-two-year-old supplied the fourth weapon that

Harris and Klebold used to storm the hallways of Columbine High School.

- Michael Carneal robbed a next-door neighbor and his own parents for his arsenal before killing three and wounding five in Paducah, Kentucky.

Many of these killers were very creative in amassing their arsenals of destruction. According to legal experts, Eric Harris and Dylan Klebold broke at least twenty existing federal and state gun laws before and during their murderous binge.[13] An interesting report was released by the Bureau of Alcohol, Tobacco and Firearms in January 1999:

- Only 35% of the guns juveniles used in crimes were stolen.
- 33% to 50% of guns used by teenage shooters were bought from licensed dealers by someone acting as a "straw" intermediary, such as a girlfriend or an illegal gun trafficker.[14]

Another problem we are dealing with is the overwhelming number of guns—more than 200 million estimated in circulation in the United States.[15] Though many of these are for hunting or protection, it is hard to keep them effectively locked away from or inaccessible to children.

O Canada!

Our friends to the north have a much better record on gun-related homicides. This is due in part to the infamous "Montreal Massacre." In 1989, a young man opened fire in a University of Montreal classroom and shot twenty-seven people, killing fourteen of them before committing suicide. This triggered a dramatic crackdown on gun ownership across Canada, which continues tightening to this day. *Star Tribune* (Minneapolis) national correspondent Bob von Sternburg says, "Compared with the United States, Canada's long history of tight gun regulation has been accompanied by far less carnage."[16]

Why are attitudes so different north of the border? The reasons are both political and cultural. It is easier, for example, to control guns in a country that has relatively few people to begin with and where firearms owners are a proportionately less potent political force.

During a recent speech in St. Paul, Minnesota, former Prime Minister Kim Campbell joked that many Canadians wouldn't mind becoming part of the United States "as long as you let us keep our health care and gun control laws."[17]

Campbell was Canada's justice minister at the time of the Montreal Massacre. Her legislation included:

- Banning semiautomatic weapons that could be converted to full automatic.

- Prohibiting the sale of guns to people under age eighteen.
- Increased screening for Canadians who applied to purchase firearms.
- Requirements that guns be stored unloaded and with a trigger lock in place.[18]

After random killings in Ottawa and Toronto in 1994, there was a renewed call for further restrictions. A new law was passed in Canada in 1995 which included:

- A blanket ban on semiautomatic assault weapons and small-caliber handguns.
- Licensing of gun owners.
- Controls on the sale of ammunition.
- Registration of Canada's 1.3 million firearms by the end of 2002.[19]

Nothing so far-reaching exists in the United States. Even the gun-control provisions recently proposed by the Clinton administration don't come close to the solemn approach taken in Canada. Most of the U.S. gun restrictions are imposed at the state or local level. Federal regulation has been scant, with the notable exceptions of the Gun Control Act of 1968 (following the assassinations of Robert F. Kennedy and Martin Luther King) and the Brady law (following the attempted assassination of President Ronald Reagan). One analyst notes: "As the gulf between gun laws in the United States and Canada has widened, so has the violence caused by guns."[20]

Murder and robbery rates when guns are used have long been lower in Canada. But for more than a decade, Canada's rates have been dropping or leveling off while the U.S. rates have been climbing. Numbers compiled by the Canada's Firearms Center show that between 1987 and 1996, the homicide rate in the United States was 8.8 per 100,000 people. It was a mere 2.3 per 100,000 in Canada.[21] Here's another way to look at it with a few other countries thrown in for comparison:

Country	*Households with Firearms*	*Gun Homicides (per million)*	*Gun Suicides (per million)*
Japan	0.6%	0.3	0.04
Netherlands	1.9%	2.7	2.8
Australia	16.0%	5.6	23.8
Canada	26.0%	6.0	33.5
United States	41.0%	62.4	72.3[22]

Two statistics here are rather remarkable. The U.S. has ten times as many gun homicides and more than twice as many gun suicides as Canada! And the survey is arranged in an "apples vs. apples" comparative analysis. The argument about the difference in size between the two countries is irrelevant. The bottom line seems pretty clear: More gun control means less homicide and suicide. Canada's got this one right.

Writing in *Time*, Margaret Carlson took this bull by the horns:

> Without guns, Eric Harris and Dylan Klebold were menacing misfits in trench coats feasting on Internet swill. With guns, they became merciless mass murderers. We're hungry for a politician who can stand up to the gun lobby and convince it that burying Isaiah Shoels last Thursday in the graduation gown he would have worn to his commencement this month is unacceptable in a civilized society.[23]

Did the abuse of the First and Second Amendments to the Constitution of the United States *cause* the school yard shooters to inflict the murder and mayhem on their communities between 1997 and 1999? No. Causation is not the debate here.

But when people take the freedom of speech and the right to bear arms to an obscene extreme, we can expect dire consequences for our society. Music, movies, television and video games will continue to contain violence that "is used primarily to invite the viewer to enjoy the feel of killing, beating, and mutilating."[24] There will continue to be too many guns available to too many teens who simply must prove a point.

And the helicopters will circle another school building somewhere in America where another gunman has decided to play *Doom* for real.

Part 3

The Supernatural Cure

"A sense of reverence for life, a connection to something deeper and higher than themselves, a core meaning in their [the boys'] hearts helps stop them from being drawn to the dark side." [1]

—Dr. James Garbarino, author of *Lost Boys*

The last several chapters have been somewhat depressing from the standpoint that most of us may feel that little will really change. We fear that the massacre at Columbine High School will be forgotten over time—at least until the next bloody episode. The right to have an abortion seems like it is here to stay for the foreseeable future. Will parents really begin to spend more time talking with their kids, or will we just go back to our busy lives and leave the kids alone with TV, video games and an unsupervised Internet?

Will the game-makers actually heed the warnings that are blaring from the blood of the slain students, or will they continue to pursue profit as the ultimate aim? Can Hollywood and the television industry truly clean up their acts and begin to produce entertainment that refuses to glorify gore and revere rage? Can we count on musicians to stop fanning the flames of suicide and destruction? Is it realistic to hope that the Internet will become regulated to some level of sanity? Will we come to a consensus on what limitations must be placed on "freedom of expression" if we are going to avert more disasters?

Not according to Brian Helgeland, who directed the ultraviolent movie *Payback,* starring Mel Gibson. "I wouldn't know how to respond to a code or consensus as to what's responsible and what isn't acceptable. That is only for me to answer in my mind."[2]

None of this sounds very hopeful.

But there is a solution to the cause of causes. That is the focus of the rest of this book. As you read on, you will begin to see that there is hope for every problem we have encountered in our culture. Though Dr. Garbarino does not take it quite far enough, he is right—troubled boys need to connect with something that is deeper and higher than themselves. In fact, all of us troubled human beings must do this. Join me as we explore this pathway.

Chapter 17

The Victor over Violence

"He was wounded and crushed for our sins. He was beaten that we might have peace."

—Isaiah 53:5

Many years ago a man and his pregnant wife went on a trip. She was closer to giving birth than either of them had thought when they left. It wasn't long before they realized that the child was on the way and they should get to a hospital. But the nearest one was more than 100 miles away, so they checked into a few motels along the road. No vacancies. Finally a farmer had mercy on them and offered a barn, some clean blankets and fresh straw.

And so it was that their son was born while curious farm animals looked on. Even though it was a humble beginning, the parents were quite sure that this boy would grow up to have a big impact on the world.

There was just something about him. They knew that he was very special.

The boy's childhood years were unremarkable except for one startling incident. When he was twelve years old, he disappeared for three days. His parents searched frantically in every direction, but he could not be found. Following up a tip from friends, they went downtown and found their son in a rather unusual setting. There he was sitting with a group of pastors at a ministerial meeting! These religious leaders were discussing deep theological issues with this twelve-year-old! It was obvious that he was conversant and far beyond his chronological age in spiritual understanding.

For eighteen years after this incident, the son worked side-by-side with his father in the family lumber business. He became a skilled carpenter. His parents knew that he would someday leave them to fulfill his own mission in life, but they were happy to have him at home for that time.

Then it happened. At the age of thirty, he stepped out on his own in a big way. He had known all along what his mission would be. He had entered the world to proclaim the good news of God's great love for the human race.

It began with a well-publicized baptism in a river. The news media swarmed this event because of the reputation of the one doing the baptizing. His name was John, and he had been a very colorful and controversial preacher in his own right. But John seemed in awe of this man, and that made it all the more intriguing.

Following his baptism, the man vanished into the wilderness for a forty-day fast. It was reported that he confronted the devil himself during that time, and he not only survived the encounter—he was the clear victor. When he returned, he was even more determined to fulfill his mission.

Over the next three years, he developed quite a following. Incredible miracles took place almost everywhere he went. He gave sermons that were unlike anything anyone had ever heard. His words carried the weight of authority and everyone who heard him was keenly aware of that fact. He made the bold claim that he was the only one who could enable people to get right with God. In fact, he claimed to be the actual Son of God, who could forgive sins.

But the very ones that should have been excited about and committed to this spiritual leader—priests and religious teachers—became disillusioned with him. They could not accept his claims to be God's Son and the promised Messiah. So they began to plot ways to discredit him. They drew him into public debates but he always made them look silly. They tried to plant rumors about his associations with questionable characters by ridiculing him as "the friend of sinners." But the crowds only grew larger.

It became clear that the only way to deal with this "false prophet" was by doing away with him altogether. A plot to murder him was hatched. They trumped up accusations of heresy. They told the political leaders that he had threatened their authority by claiming that he was the supreme ruler of a kingdom that would never end. By the time of the trial, the fix was in. The judge himself tried to offer a plea of "not guilty by reason of insanity" on his behalf. But the jury was determined. The death penalty was issued. Within hours he was brutally beaten and then nailed to a cross. He died several painful hours later.

No one ever stopped to think about the insane irony of the situation. This man had preached peace and love. He was not interested in political power or influence. His mission was to give people an opportunity to have a personal relationship with God. He had been completely misunderstood and misrepresented. He had never broken even one law and yet he received the harshest penalty the law could offer. A life devoted to promoting reconciliation ended in the most sadistic kind of violence and bloodshed.

However, something very strange happened just a few days after he had been removed from the cross and given a proper burial. Even though the graveyard was heavily guarded and his tomb had been completely secured, rumors began to circulate that he had come back to life. Some even claimed to have seen the open tomb with no body inside! Eventually hundreds of witnesses came forward to say that they had seen him walking and talking with his followers.

His name, of course, is Jesus. You have just read a brief paraphrase of the Gospel accounts (Matthew, Mark, Luke, John) of His birth, life, death and resurrection.

Crushed for Our Sins

So far this book has been about some very bad news: all of us were born with a sinful nature. This fallen character is the cause of causes for all of the evil behavior in our world. Essentially, this is why kids kill. It is why adults kill. It also explains why humans in general struggle with things like hate, lust, envy, gossip, slander, adultery, addictions (gambling, food, drugs, alcohol, tobacco) and so many other vices.

When sin entered the human race, along with it came consequences that affect us spiritually, emotionally and physically:

- Spiritually, sin has separated us from God and the ability to find a meaningful, joyful existence. "Your sins have cut you off from God" (Isaiah 59:2).
- Emotionally, sin results in depression, anxiety and a host of other psychological complications. In our state of separation from God, we cannot enjoy the blessings expressed by Isaiah the prophet: "You will keep in perfect peace all who trust in you, whose thoughts are fixed on you!" (Isaiah 26:3).

- Physically, sin affects our bodies with strange diseases, the aging process and eventually death. God said to Eve: "You will bear children with intense pain and suffering" (Genesis 3:16). God said to Adam: "You will return to the ground from which you came. For you were made from dust, and to the dust you will return" (Genesis 3:19).

The Creator resolved this enormous sin problem and its overwhelming consequences with a radical solution. He sent His one and only Son, Jesus Christ, to become the sacrifice for our sins: "For God made Christ, who never sinned, to be the offering for our sin, so that we could be made right with God through Christ" (2 Corinthians 5:21).

Think about this: Jesus took all of the vicious acts of every human being upon Himself when He died in such violence on the cross. The Bible says that God poured all of our unrighteousness into Christ so that He could pour all of Christ's righteousness into us. What an incredible achievement on our behalf! He Who knew no sin became sin for us!

When the Lord Jesus died, He took upon Himself all of the murders of Stalin, Hitler, Mussolini and other brutal dictators. Had these men turned to God for His pardon, even on their deathbeds, they would have been completely forgiven for their innumerable sins. The savagery of Eric Harris, Dylan Klebold and all of the other teen killers was also heaped upon Christ as He hung on that cross. This kind of identification with our sin-sick souls is truly incomprehensible.

Jesus became our substitute. This is the essence of the concept of sacrifice. Christ died in our place. He became our lawyer, representing our case before His Father: "There is someone to plead for you before the Father. He is Jesus Christ, the one who pleases God completely. He is the sacrifice for our sins. He takes away not only our sins but the sins of all the world" (1 John 2:1-2).

Let this reality sink in. We were utterly lost, without God and without hope. We had committed transgressions too numerous to mention, and we had no way to escape the vicious sin cycle. We were under thick, dense clouds of guilt, unable to see the light. Then Jesus became our sin-bearer. And the consequences for Him were enormous.

Hell to Pay

The just punishment for our rebellion would have been eternity separated from the presence of a holy God. In short, we had hell to pay for our wanton sinfulness. This would have been justice. But instead we got mercy. The Savior accepted hell in our place. So for the first time ever, Christ addressed His Father impersonally as He slowly died on the cross. He referred to Him remotely as "My God." He cried out over and over from His painful perch: "My God, my God, why have you forsaken me?" (Matthew 27:46).

This was the very essence of damnation—to be separated from the Creator. Jesus entered into that dark experience of ultimate misery so that you and I would never have to be cut off in that way. The Savior made a way for all of us to get back into a right relationship with God. He opened the door to our forgiveness for every past, present or future sin. By taking our transgressions upon Himself, Christ enabled us to come before a holy God with clean hearts.

No Greater Love

Why was Jesus willing to bear our sins and be separated from His Father on our behalf? One word says it all: love.

"For God so loved the world that he gave his only Son, so that everyone who believes in him will not perish but have eternal life" (John 3:16).

"The greatest love is shown when people lay down their lives for their friends" (John 15:13).

> Oh, the love that drew salvation's plan!
> Oh, the grace that brought it down to man!
> Oh, the mighty gulf that God did span
> At Calvary!
> Mercy there was great, and grace was free;
> Pardon there was multiplied to me;
> There my burdened soul found liberty—
> At Calvary.[1]

So many people in our world today have the feeling that "nobody loves me." There is so much abuse and neglect. Children are tossed back and forth between divorced parents who don't love each other anymore. Spouses are physically beaten or emotionally battered. Humans everywhere are looking for real love—and usually in the wrong places. But there is no greater love than that which has been offered to all of us by Jesus Christ.

My heart aches for the lost boys who have murdered classmates and teachers. If only Dylan Klebold and Eric Harris could have known and accepted the deep love of Jesus. If they had only realized that Christ accepted them completely, just as they were. The Savior could fully sympathize with the way in which these boys felt rejected by their peers. Jesus knew the pain and loneliness of being an outsider.

Although we may question his motives for saying so in prison, convicted school shooter Luke Woodham was right when he said: "I know I did some bad things. This would not have happened if I had had God in my life."[2]

The Only Way

We love our religious options in North America. Many would agree with James Kullander. As a graduate student at Union Theological Seminary in New York, he wrote a piece for the *New York Times* entitled, "God, on Our Own Terms":

> It doesn't matter what people turn to in their spiritual search, be it Christian mysticism or spiritual traditions like Buddhism, Hinduism and Native American spirituality. What matters is the search itself because that—if charted according to one's deepest psychic needs—is what will eventually give life meaning. Many New Age seekers are trying to reinvigorate Christianity and keep it from becoming obsolete. Asking people today to believe solely in the traditional version of Christianity shaped by people who lived 2,000 years ago is like asking them to believe that the world is flat.[3]

If we accept Mr. Kullander's view, then we must ask these hard questions in regard to statements made and actions taken by Jesus Christ:

Was Jesus lying when He dogmatically claimed to be the exclusive way to enter into a meaningful relationship with His Father? And if He falsified that extraordinary assertion, is Christ worthy of any kind of worship at all? Why build an entire religion around a prevaricator?

If Jesus knew that He would only be one option in the religious supermarket, why would He go to such extremes with His bloody crucifixion and dramatic resurrection? Why not just be another Muhammad or L. Ron Hubbard? Why not just walk peacefully among us like these men did for awhile, offering moral and metaphysical lessons, and then die quietly like the other spiritual gurus?

Consider the immensely restrictive statement that the Lord Jesus made about Himself: "I am the way, the truth, and the life. No one can come to the Father except through me" (John 14:6).

There are no loopholes here. Jesus offers no other possible alternative. He does not present Himself as one of the ways, one of the truths or one of the sources of life. It is a rather blunt, unqualified statement about the singular pathway to a personal relationship with God. He drew a line in the spiritual sands of time: "Cross this line with Me, and I will take you to My Father and I will give you abundant life both here and hereafter. Stay behind the line and you will be forever separated from My Father, and you will suffer death both here and hereafter."

Is this radical? Indeed.

Is it simple to understand? Oh, yes.

Is it difficult to follow? Certainly.

Is it worth it? Completely.

Is it true? Absolutely.

How to Receive the Gift of Salvation

Have you responded to the love and grace of Jesus Christ with regard to your own sin problem? Have you ever asked the Savior to forgive your sins, cleanse your heart and take control of your life? There could be no better time to do such a thing than right now. The Lord Jesus stands ready to hear your confession.

The following words do not represent some "magic potion," but if you will pray something like this from a sincere heart, the Lord will answer. You can join the family of God and enjoy the freedom of forgiveness and the promise of eternal life. Here's a prayer you could use:

Dear Lord Jesus,

I know that I am a sinner. I believe that You alone are the Savior. Please forgive my sins and come into my heart. Help me to live for You. Thanks for doing what You promised.

If you prayed this prayer for the very first time, inviting Christ to become your Savior, I would like to send you something to help you live a Christian life and grow in the Christian faith. Please complete the form at the back of this book.

For those who just prayed this prayer, let me be the first to say, "Welcome to the family of God!" You have just dealt with the core issue of life on this earth and eternity beyond this world. This is the most important decision you have ever made. One day at a time, Jesus will begin to change you from the inside out. You will begin to notice the difference immediately in some areas. Though filled with challenges, the Christian life is truly the abundant life.

The next chapter is important for old and new believers alike. How can we deal with Satan as children of God?

Chapter 18

The Devil's Defeat: Then, Now and Forever

"I stand for believing in God and defying the devil—and our God loves that kind of courage among His people."[1]

—Dr. A.W. Tozer

Eric Harris and Dylan Klebold had intended to kill as many as 500 people during their bloody rage in Littleton, Colorado. However, their rampage ended far short of this terrifying plan. Why? Some might point to the fact that the boys knew they were surrounded by hundreds of heavily armed law enforcement agents. But they still had plenty of bombs and ammunition for their guns. Murdering a few dozen cops could have been a grand finale to their deadly day. Perhaps something else was going on upstairs in that school.

Dan Mayhew of The Summit Fellowships in Portland, Oregon came up with a spine-tingling theory as he reflected on those last moments before everything got quiet again in the library at Columbine High on April 20, 1999:

> I was meditating on the passage in Revelation that speaks of the forces of darkness being overcome by the people of God through "the blood of the Lamb, the word of their testimony, and they did not love their lives even unto death." I think of Cassie [Bernall], whose testimony, and the commitment of her life, stood against the attackers. Is there any way of knowing how long after Cassie's statement of faith the attack ended? Was she the last to die before the gunmen? Could the demonic inspiration for the attack have been overcome just as the Revelation passage described?[2]

It is my firm belief that Mr. Mayhew is on to something inspiring and remarkable here. Although the diary of Eric Harris indicates that suicide was to be the deadly duo's final act, the timing of it is extremely suspect. In a way, these mass murderers were just getting started when things came to a rather abrupt halt. It is difficult to come up with any hypothesis from the natural world that would explain the decision of Klebold and Harris to end it all when they did.

Looking at this from a supernatural perspective, allow me to reconstruct what most likely happened in the moments before the bodies of the gunmen collapsed to the floor:

Gunman [to Cassie Bernall]: "Do you believe in God?"

Cassie [after hesitating momentarily]: "Yes, I believe in God."

Gunman: "Why?" [Shoots Cassie without giving her a chance to answer][3]

Something happened at that very moment which changed everything. The devil was soundly defeated in that moment of martyrdom—by the blood of the Lamb; through the word of Cassie's testimony; because she was not afraid to die (Revelation 12:11). Satan had met his match. There was nothing left for him to do but surrender. Lucifer's final pernicious deed was to inspire the death of his hosts. Eric Harris and Dylan Klebold obliged their master by taking aim at themselves and pulling the triggers.

I am convinced that many lives were saved when this power encounter with darkness ended in victory for Almighty God. Had Cassie Bernall and the other Columbine martyrs denied their faith in that crucial moment, the powerful grip of the prince of darkness would have only intensified. Many others, including police and rescue workers, would have been massacred.

Satan's Defeat

Unlike the Lord Jesus Christ, whose rule shall never end, the devil is on a deadline. There is a day coming when he will no longer roam about, seeking whom he may devour. Satan received his death sentence on the cross and at the empty tomb. But that verdict will not be finally and forever executed until the end of time. Jesus dogmatically declared the devil's demise when He spoke of ". . . the eternal fire prepared for the Devil and his demons!" (Matthew 25:41).

We should note here that hellfire was prepared for the devil and his demons. Our God, full of grace and mercy, is not willing that even one human being should perish in this awful place (2 Peter 3:9). We have to choose this for ourselves by willfully rejecting His love and salvation.

John joins in with the joyful celebration of Lucifer's eternal destruction: "Then the Devil, who betrayed them, was thrown into the lake of fire that burns with sulfur, joining the beast and the false prophet. There they will be tormented day and night forever and ever" (Revelation 20:10).

This is the devil's defeat—then, now and for eternity.

Periodically God puts on display a depiction of what lies ahead for the enemy. It is a demonstration of how the Almighty always ultimately wins. This happened most recently in a library at a high school in Colorado. Just when Satan thought he had God against the ropes, everything was quickly turned around. Revival came from a rampage.

Chapter 19

Revival from a Rampage

"If the killers gave evil a face, the victims lent theirs to grace. In ever-widening circles the story that lingers is the tale of Cassie Bernall, the girl who when asked 'Do you believe in God?' was murdered when she said yes. We expect our martyrs to be etched in stained glass, not carrying a backpack." [1]

—Nancy Gibbs in *Time*

The scene in the library at Columbine High School in the early hours of the afternoon on April 20, 1999 must have been horrible beyond description. At first glance, it appeared to be nothing but carnage and confusion. Death and destruction unfolded in every direction. Mutilated bodies lay limp and lifeless. Splattered blood covered the floors and tables.

The devil had clearly been in charge there—wasn't he? He could declare a huge victory—couldn't he?

This was one of Satan's finest hours—wasn't it? The answers will surprise you.

The Story That Lingers

The opening quotation from *Time* columnist Nancy Gibbs makes an interesting point. "The story that lingers" is not the reporting on the gunmen or their parents. It's not the sensational murder and mayhem that took place. All the coverage about the school, the administrators, the police, the weapons and a hundred other related matters is fading away. Our nation has already begun to focus its short attention span on more current events. But one aspect of this incident simply will not go away.

Six weeks after the shootings, an article in *USA Today* entitled "17-year-old's last words inspire other Christians" made this bold declaration: "A simple affirmation of religious faith, uttered in the last moments of her life, is turning a 17-year-old victim of the Columbine High School massacre into a modern-day martyr."[2]

Eileen McNamara, writing for the *Boston Globe*, voiced a similar theme as she visited Littleton just four days after the massacre:

> More than any other image from this scene of carnage—more than the flowers deep as the snow in Clement Park, more than the blue and silver ribbons on every lapel—the most affecting is the sight

> of strapping young men and gracious young women on their knees in prayer everywhere one looks in this prairie suburb at the foothills of the Rocky Mountains.[3]

This is the story that lingers. Revival has sprung forth from a rampage! With remarkable courage and conviction, Cassie Bernall and two other classmates passed the ultimate test of their faith in the most demanding setting that could be imagined. In the words of *Time* magazine, these teenage girls "triumphantly sustained their confession in the face of the ultimate peer pressure—the barrel of a gun."[4]

Let's take a closer look at the harbingers of this renewal—two martyrs and one who survived.

"For this reason, Cassie was born"

Just two years ago, Cassie Bernall was on several prayer lists. She had fallen in with the wrong crowd. Her main concerns at the time were keeping her weight down, being attractive for the boys and being popular. Cassie delved into drugs, dabbled in the occult and had a fascination with suicide. Her exasperated parents, Brad and Misty, moved her into a Christian school and sent her to West Bowles Community Church.

Under protest Cassie joined the church's youth group. After his first meeting with this young woman, youth minister Dave McPherson said, "I never gave Cassie a hope. She was disconnected. She wasn't going to listen to anything. She was into black magic, the dark stuff."[5]

Many, however, prayed earnestly for Cassie. Six months later at a Christian camp, she accepted Christ, and an amazing transformation took place. The sullen, introverted girl became a bright, happy young lady with boundless energy. She insisted on leaving the security of her Christian school so that she could become a witness to others.

And that's exactly what happened. Cassie became an effective evangelist on the Columbine campus. She carried her Bible frequently and unashamedly and was known for her WWJD? ("What Would Jesus Do?") bracelet. Though she had her doubts and fears like anyone else, she allowed her faith in Jesus to keep her steady. That firm foundation gave her strength at the moment she needed it the most.

The exact exchange of words between the gunmen and Cassie Bernall is not known. There were obviously no audio or video records. Those who witnessed the conversation were so traumatized at the moment that their accounts would understandably vary. Here are the three versions I have come across in my research:

Version #1

Gunman: "Do you believe in God?"

Cassie: "Yes, I believe."

Gunman: "Why?" (She is killed before she can answer.)

Version #2

Gunman: "Do you believe in God?"

Cassie: "Yes, I believe in God."

Gunman: "There is no God."

Cassie: "There is a God, and you need to follow His path." (She is then killed.)

Version #3

Gunman: "Do you believe in God?"

Cassie: "Yes, I believe in God." (She is then killed.)

We should not be too concerned with getting the precise words used in this dialogue. The important point is that when Cassie Bernall was asked to stand for her faith in Jesus Christ, she did so with the full awareness that it could result in her execution. As classmate Mickie Cain told Larry King on CNN, "She completely stood up for God. When the killers asked her if there was anyone who had faith in Christ, she spoke up and they shot her for it."[6]

On the night of her death, Cassie's brother Chris found a poem she had written just two days before her promotion to Paradise:

Now I have given up on everything else
I have found it to be the only way
To really know Christ and experience
The mighty power that brought Him back to life again,
and to find

Out what it means to suffer and to Die with Him.
So, whatever it takes I will be one who lives in the fresh
Newness of life of those who are Alive from the dead.[7]

The last assignment Cassie completed on this earth was a reading which was supposed to be discussed at a youth group meeting on the evening of April 20, 1999. The book was called *Seeking Peace.* Ms. Bernall had underlined a passage from Martin Luther King Jr.: "If a man hasn't found something he will die for, he isn't fit to live."[8]

Cassie was not able to attend that youth group meeting. She had already been promoted to the ultimate peace in eternity with her Lord. But her death brought abundant spiritual life. According to youth workers who attended her memorial service, there were at least seventy-five conversion commitments to Christ because of Cassie Bernall's willingness to die for her faith. Broadcast internationally by CNN and other major channels, only God knows the full impact of this young lady's martyrdom, which opened the door to new life for so many.

Dr. Ed Tropp, Associate Pastor of Circle Drive Baptist Church in Colorado Springs, Colorado, reports that Cassie's courage has led many Christian teens to repent of their spiritual apathy. Two backslidden students survived the massacre in the library, but they saw the boldness of those who died for their belief in God. When they came out, they vowed to never again compromise their Christianity as long as they live. This is a recurring theme in youth groups around the country: the martyrdom of these teens has emboldened those who had been shy and shallow in their commitment to Christ.

The reaction of Cassie's parents was illuminating. Brad Bernall said, "It is clear to me that this tragic incident has been thrown back into the face of Satan and his followers with an impact that is much greater than what was intended for us, God's children."[9]

On her casket he wrote a note to Cassie which said, "I can't wait until we are reunited in heaven. I am proud of the way you made your stand.—Daddy."[10]

Cassie's mother, Misty, told a friend that God spoke clearly to her shortly after her daughter's death, saying, "For this reason, Cassie was born."[11] Mrs. Bernall is writing a book entitled, *She Said Yes: The Unlikely Martyrdom of Cassie Bernall* (scheduled for release by Plough Publishing in September 1999). Unlikely martyrdom indeed! This child of Satan became a child of God and died because she declared her spiritual allegiance!

Reporting from Fort Lauderdale, Florida, *USA Today* detailed the impact that the death of Cassie Bernall was having around the country. Her willingness to take a stand for Christ has galvanized believers in a unique and powerful way. Cassie's final words in this world—"Yes, I believe in God"—have been broadcast from countless pulpits. They are plastered on T-shirts and lapel buttons.

Rallies have been held in Bernall's honor in Florida, Colorado, Illinois, Pennsylvania and California. Twenty-two more were planned for the summer of 1999. Several Internet sites have been devoted to this young martyr. Although songs, CDs and angel pins have been created to capitalize on the courage of Cassie, many in her generation are rejecting attempts to commercialize her memory. "We don't want her message to be sensationalized or abused in any way," said Josh Weidmann, seventeen, a member of a Denver-based Bible study group called Revival Generation. "It's not so much what Cassie said. It's what we are going to say when we're asked the question."[12]

Police officer Wayne Depew walked among the corpses in the library at Columbine High. He saw Cassie Bernall's body lying lifeless under a table. At first he didn't notice the bullet hole in her temple, but he saw her hands clasped as if in prayer. "She had a real soft look on her face, with a slight smile."[13]

That's the smile of someone who has just heard Jesus say, "Well done, my good and faithful servant" (Matthew 25:23).

"Then go be with him now!"

Rachel Scott attended the youth group at Orchard Road Christian Center, an Assemblies of God church with a membership of over 3,000. She was also active at Cellebration Christian Center. Rachel was a deeply committed believer who wanted to go into missionary work in Africa. The details of her martyrdom did not become known until two weeks after the Columbine massacre.

When Eric Harris and Dylan Klebold entered the school, Rachel Scott was sitting with a boy outside the cafeteria. The shooters approached them both and shot her first—in the leg. The boy fled, but he was gunned down and presumed dead. However, he survived. But when Klebold and Harris turned their attention back to Ms. Scott, they confronted the high-profile believer about her faith. From my reading of David Van Biema's article in *Time,*[14] I would reconstruct the conversation and execution as follows:

The shooter leaned over her crippled body and whispered, "Do you believe in God?"

Rachel responded, "Yes."

The gunmen replied, "Then go be with him now!"

Rachel was then shot in the head. She died instantly.

Over 3,000 attended Rachel Scott's funeral which was also broadcast live on CNN. Millions of people around the world were watching as God got the glory for this young woman's courageous death. Pastor Bruce Porter made this salient comment: "Prayer was reestablished in our public schools last Tuesday. What the judiciary couldn't do, what the churches couldn't do, the children did themselves."[15]

He asked the throngs of young people gathered before him, "Rachel carried the torch of love, compassion, and good news of the Savior—who will pick it up?"[16]

Hundreds of teens raised their hands to declare their intent to follow in the brave footsteps of this seventeen-year-old martyr. At least fifteen kids embraced Christ as their Savior right there. Reports came back about young people around the nation who jumped to their feet to make that same pledge as they watched on TV. This is the lingering story out of Littleton, Colorado. A spiritual revival is underway that not only takes back the ground gained by Satan on April 20, 1999—it utterly destroys his devious long-range plot, too. Instead of more rioting on campuses, renewal is sweeping the land.

Rachel's father, Darrell Scott, in a powerful speech to the House Subcommittee on Crime, said:

> I am here today to declare that Columbine was not just a tragedy—it was a spiritual event that should be forcing us to look at where the real blame lies! Much of that blame lies here in this room.

> Much of that blame lies behind the pointing fingers of the accusers themselves.[17]

Then he quoted a poem he penned on May 23, 1999:

> Your laws ignore our deepest needs
> Your words are empty air
> You've stripped away our heritage
> You've outlawed simple prayer.
> Now gunshots fill our classrooms
> And precious children die
> You seek for answers everywhere
> And ask the question "WHY?"
> You regulate restrictive laws
> Through legislative creed
> And yet you fail to understand
> That God is what we need![18]

Pointing to the revival that is already underway, Scott concluded with these words of hope: "My daughter's death will not be in vain. The young people of this country will not allow that to happen."[19]

"Divine Intervention"

Valeen Schnurr faced the same life-and-death question that confronted Rachel Scott and Cassie Bernall. She was hiding under a table with Lauren Townsend when Harris and Klebold marched into the library. They walked right by them and threw a pipe bomb into another section of the room causing books to fly in every direction. As the gunmen began shooting other students, Valeen could hear the cries for mercy as classmates were pleading for their lives. She witnessed the martyrdom of Cassie Bernall.

Screams from her side of the room led Eric and Dylan back in her direction with guns blazing. They shot under Ms. Schnurr's table and struck both Valeen and Lauren. Lauren died immediately. Valeen clutched her abdomen, which had been pelted with bullets and shrapnel. The following dialogue then ensued:

> Valeen: "Oh my God, oh my God."
> Gunman: "God?! Do you really believe in God?"
> Valeen: "Yes, I believe in God."
> Gunman: "Why?" (The gunman had paused to reload)
> Valeen: "I do believe in God, and my mom and dad taught me about God."[20]

She remembers babbling on a little longer and then crawling away under another table. At that point Eric Harris and Dylan Klebold left that area of the room and never returned. Crawling away may have saved her life. She later told her mother that she was terrified to confirm her belief in God because she had seen what happened to Cassie Bernall. But she was able to take courage from Cassie's bold testimony.

When it was over, Valeen held the hand of Lauren Townsend. She touched her face and told her to wake up—it was time to escape. Wrapping her sweatshirt tightly around her own bullet-riddled stomach, Valeen even tried to carry Lauren out. But she was just too weak from her voluminous loss of blood.

Valeen Schnurr miraculously survived nine bullet and shrapnel wounds down the left side of her body. Paramedics had told her parents that they did not expect her to live. Doctors at Swedish Medical Center attributed her survival and remarkably rapid recovery to "divine intervention," according to Valeen's mother.

So . . . Who Won in Littleton?

At the beginning of this chapter, I told you that the answer to this question would surprise you. Here it is: The devil and his forces of darkness were convincingly defeated on April 20, 1999 at Columbine High School. Littleton will not ultimately be remembered for the rampage of Dylan Klebold and Eric Harris. Instead, this event will be commemorated for the revival that sprung forth from the blood of martyrs.

Scores of young people have entered the family of God through this terrifying incident. Lucifer's fury burned brightly—but only briefly in those hallways and classrooms. In the aftermath, God is still on His throne, and Paradise has been enriched by the presence of Rachel Scott, Cassie Bernall and other believers who were killed during this satanic blitzkrieg.

How many lives were impacted by the faithfulness of these martyrs? We will have to wait to receive that answer someday in heaven.

There is a sense in which the halls of Columbine High School are holy ground. It was there that a fierce battle took place between Almighty God and His archenemy, the devil. Two boys had sold their souls to Satan. They appeared to have the advantage over two frightened teenage girls. Both of these young women were asked to renounce their faith in Christ under the deadly glare of a gun barrel. Heaven and hell awaited their confession.

Both in the hallway and in the library, the answer came back the same: "Yes, I believe in God!" The horrifying hail of bullets that followed those daring declarations was not the end of the story. It was, in fact, the beginning of a movement that will no doubt grow deeper and wider until Jesus Christ returns to set everything straight once and for all.

Revival from a rampage. It's a God thing.

Epilogue

The Final Solution

"He will remove all of their sorrows, and there will be no more death or sorrow or crying or pain. For the old world and its evils are gone forever."

—Revelation 21:4

One thing is crystal clear to anyone who has read this book: We live in a dangerous and deadly world. Those who fled the inner city to find safety and security in the suburbs have had a rude awakening. People who assumed that rural communities would provide a refuge from the ravages of violence have been shocked to see young gunmen storming their schools.

So I have some bad news and some good news.

The bad news is that the murder and mayhem will get much worse before it gets eternally better. There are several reasons for this. America is like many great athletes, actors and businesspeople who climbed out of poverty and oppression to become multimillionaires. They simply could not handle the incredible, instant wealth and the vast number of temptations that came with it.

In the same way, our unrestrained freedoms will be our undoing. Consider the explosive ingredients in this lethal stew:

- It begins with humans who are born with a sinful nature. Our inclination is toward evil, not righteousness. We don't "become" bad—we start out that way.
- These fallen beings teach others that they evolved from a chance meeting of chemicals in a primordial pool billions of years ago. The message is that our lives have about as much meaning as a snail.
- So next we give these human beings the freedom to abort another human being. This sends the unmistakable message that life is cheap.
- Then we add an almost unlimited right to "free speech." Movies, music and video games can be packed with gratuitous violence because the "artists" who created them must be at liberty to express themselves without fear of any censorship.
- And of course we should be at liberty to own guns with very few restrictions. The market becomes flooded with cheap "Saturday Night Special" handguns. Assault rifles are imported and then protected for the purpose of "hunting."

> Surprise of surprises, violent deaths by firearms begin to rise at alarming rates!

This pathetic pattern isn't going to change anytime soon. Yes, there is plenty of posturing in the various media right now, but they will get over the latest school massacre because the customers will get over it. They will go right back to producing whatever sells because they are driven by greed instead of godliness. There will be tough talk about new gun control measures, but there are too many guns for any number of new laws to control.

Now for some good news.

God Is Still in Control

As we contemplate the carnage of recent years, particularly among our youth, it may appear that the Creator has simply "left the building." This is not the case at all. Though God takes no pleasure in the violence that is sweeping our land, He has allowed it to illustrate the principle that we reap what we have sown. His warning is unambiguous: "Don't be misled. Remember that you can't ignore God and get away with it. You will always reap what you sow!" (Galatians 6:7).

The Creator's ultimate control of this situation can be seen in the way He is using the martyrdom of two precious Christian girls to spark a nationwide renewal. How wonderful to hear the gospel being preached on CNN worldwide at the memorial services! People who would have never tuned in to a Billy Graham Crusade on television were introduced to the claims of Jesus Christ in a dramatic setting that they will not soon forget.

A.W. Tozer reminds us that God is never surprised by things such as the school shootings that have occurred the past few years. "Because God knows all things perfectly, He knows no thing better than any other thing, but all things equally well. He never discovers anything, He is never surprised, never amazed. He never wonders about anything."[1]

Remember—God is in control. One grand day is ahead that will establish His dominion for all eternity.

The Day of the Lord

Hitler had his day. Eric Harris, Dylan Klebold and the school murderers before them have had their day too. But sometime, perhaps very soon, this world will experience a day like no other. Throughout the Bible it is called the day of the Lord: "The day of the Lord will come as unexpectedly as a thief. Then the heavens will pass away with a terrible noise, and everything in them will disappear in fire, and the earth and everything on it will be exposed to judgment" (2 Peter 3:10).

This is the day when everything crooked will be made straight. Final, complete justice will be carried out in the lives of every human being. Anyone who ever escaped punishment for a crime they committed because of a loophole in the law of man will be face-to-face with the Judge of all the earth:

> And I saw a great white throne, and I saw the one who was sitting on it. The earth and sky fled from his presence, but they found no place to hide. I saw the dead, both great and small, standing before God's throne. . . . And the dead were judged according to the things written in the books, according to what they had done. (Revelation 20:11-12)

No one in the human race can escape this appointment with the Almighty. Those who have accepted Jesus Christ can approach this moment with confidence because their names will be found in the Book of Life. But the nightmare of nightmares awaits those who rejected this wonderful Redeemer: "Anyone whose name was not found recorded in the Book of Life was thrown into the lake of fire" (Revelation 20:15).

I would urge anyone who has not received the gift of salvation to escape this eternal damnation by calling on the Lord Jesus Christ to forgive your sins. He will do just that. He will come into your heart and give you His peace and the assurance of life forever in the family of God (see chapter 17).

God's Final Solution

When will the violence truly come to an end? Is there a "final solution"? Consider the description of heaven in the book of Revelation:

> Then I saw a new heaven and a new earth, for the old heaven and the old earth had disappeared. And the sea was also gone. And I saw the holy city, the new Jerusalem, coming down from God. . . . "Look, the home of God is now among his people! He will live with them, and they will be his people. God himself will be with them. He will remove all of their sorrows, and there will be no more death or sorrow or crying or pain. For the old world and its evils are gone forever." (Revelation 21:1-4)

Oh happy day! God will replace this transitory world with a brand-new one. This bankrupt planet with all of its murder and mayhem will be utterly forgotten. In its place, the very glory of heaven. And this won't be a temporary fix—*it is the final solution!*

Wonderful reunions are just around the corner. The martyrs of Columbine High School will be reunited with parents and friends. Those who trusted in Christ because of their boldness in the face of death will be there rejoicing too.

No more funerals. No more tearful good-byes. No more newscasts depicting death and destruction. All of these former miseries will be gone forever. We will be together with our precious Lord for all eternity.

Thank God for His final solution. The best is yet to come!

Notes

Introduction—The Doomsday Dozen

1 Nancy Gibbs, "The Littleton Massacre," *Time*, May 3, 1999, p. 34.

Part 1—Natural Born Killers

1 Lynne Cheney, "Time Forum: Tough Talk on Entertainment," *Time*, June 12, 1995, p. 32.
2 Tim Russert, *Meet the Press*, May 9, 1999, 10 a.m. (EST).

Chapter 1—The New Profile of a Mass Murderer

1 Mass Murderer Hit List. [Online]. Available www.mayhem.net/Crime/murder1.html.
2 Ibid.
3 Ibid.
4 Bob Herbert, "Addicted to Violence," *New York Times*, April 22, 1999.

Chapter 2—Monday, Monday

1 Caitlin Lovinger, "After the Madness: Violence, Even Before the Internet," *New York Times*, April 25, 1999, section 4, p. 18.
2 *Time*, February 12, 1979, p. 25.

3 James Garbarino, *Lost Boys* (New York: The Free Press, 1999), p. 6.
4 Ibid., pp. 7, 9.
5 Lovinger, p. 18.
6 John Cloud, "Just a Routine School Shooting," *Time*, May 31, 1999, p. 36.
7 Brian Cofer, "Beyond Westside: Rash of School Shootings Across U.S. Mars '97-'98," *Arkansas Democrat-Gazette*, March 21, 1999.
8 Ibid.
9 Ibid.
10 "Teen Charged in Canada School Shooting," *Minneapolis Star Tribune*, April 30, 1999.
11 Lovinger.

Chapter 3—Gutsy and Daring

1 Howard Chua-eoan, "Six Friends Charged with Conspiracy," *Time*, October 20, 1997, p. 54.
2 Ibid.
3 "Mississippi Teen Accused of Killing 3, Injuring 7 in Rampage," *Minneapolis Star Tribune*, October 2, 1997, p. 4.
4 Bill Hewett, "The Avenger," *People*, November 3, 1997, p. 116.
5 Ibid.
6 Ibid.
7 Gina Holland, "I Am Not Insane, I Am Angry." [Online]. Available http://www.sunherald.com/new/docs/shooting1003.htm.
8 Hewett, p. 116.
9 Howard Chua-eoan, "An Alleged One-Man Rampage May Have Become a Seven-Pointed Conspiracy," *Time*, October 20, 1997, p. 54.
10 Hewett, p. 116.
11 Ibid.

12 Brian Cabell, "Pearl School Shooting Suspect Gets Life for Stabbing Mom," CNN, June 5, 1998.
13 Ibid.
14 Ibid.
15 Ibid.
16 Judith Crosson, "Teenager Blames School Shooting on Lack of Religion." [Online]. Available http://www.nandotimes.com/nation/071598/nation 12_18874_noframes.html.
17 Hewett, p. 116.

Chapter 4—Death at a Prayer Meeting

1 Jonah Blank and Warren Cohen, "Prayer Circle Murders," *U.S. News & World Report*, December 15, 1997, p. 24.
2 Julie Grace, "When the Silence Fell," *Time*, December 15, 1997, www.pathfinder.com/time/magazine/1997/dom/971215/nation.when_the_sile.html.
3 Ibid.
4 Jonah Blank, "The Kid No One Noticed," *U.S. News & World Report*, October 12, 1998, p. 27.
5 Ibid.
6 Ibid., p. 28.
7 Ibid.
8 Ibid., p. 29.
9 Ibid., p. 30.
10 Ibid., p. 27.
11 Ibid.
12 James Prichard, "Teen Enters Guilty Plea in School Shooting," *Seattle Times*, October 5, 1998.
13 Blank, p. 27.
14 Daniel Pedersen and Sarah Van Boven, "Tragedy in a Small Place," *Newsweek*, December 15, 1997, p. 30.
15 Blank and Cohen, p. 24.
16 Blank, p. 30.

Chapter 5—Lured into the Crosshairs

1 Nadya Labi, "The Hunter and the Choirboy," *Time*, April 6, 1998, p. 36.
2 Ibid., p. 29.
3 Ibid., p. 33.
4 Ibid.
5 Ibid., p. 34.
6 Ibid., p. 30.
7 Ibid., p. 34.
8 Ibid.
9 "The Lost Children: What Can We Do about It?," *Arkansas Democrat-Gazette*, March 26, 1998.
10 Kenneth Heard, "Shooter's Mom Sees Son Jailed, Innocence Lost," *Arkansas Democrat-Gazette*, March 21, 1999.
11 Charlotte Faltermayer, "What Is Justice for a Sixth-Grade Killer?," *Time*, April 6, 1998, p. 36.
12 Heard, "Shooter's Mom."
13 Faltermayer, p. 36.
14 Kenneth Heard, "Jonesboro School Shooter, 12, Plans to Appeal Guilty Ruling," *Arkansas Democrat-Gazette*, September 5, 1998.
15 "Johnson's, Golden's Parents Want Suit Against Them Dropped," *Arkansas Democrat-Gazette*, September 1, 1998.
16 Kenneth Heard, "Mom Moving Past the 'Why,' " *Arkansas Democrat-Gazette*, March 21, 1999.
17 John Deering, *Arkansas Democrat-Gazette*, March 27, 1998.
18 Richard Lacayo, "Toward the Root of the Evil," *Time*, April 6, 1998, p. 38.

Chapter 6—An All-American Kid

1 Margot Hornblower, "The Boy Who Loved Bombs," *Time*, June 1, 1998, p. 44.
2 Gordon Witkin, "Again," *U.S. News & World Report*, June 1, 1998, p. 16.

3 Debra Gwartney, "A Son Who Spun Out of Control," *Newsweek*, June 1, 1998, p. 32.
4 Hornblower, p. 44.
5 Joshua Hammer, "Kid Is Out of Control," *Newsweek*, June 8, 1998, p. 32.
6 Gwartney, p. 32.
7 Hammer, p. 33.
8 Ibid., p. 34.
9 Ibid.
10 Witkin, pp. 16-18, 21.
11 Gwartney, p. 33.
12 Witkin, p. 17.
13 Ibid.

Chapter 7—Rage in the Rockies

1 Gibbs, p. 26.
2 Ibid., p. 25.
3 Eric Pooley, "Portrait of a Deadly Bond," *Time*, May 10, 1999, p. 26.
4 Betsy Steisand and Angie Cannon, "Exorcising the Pain," *U.S. News and World Report*, May 10, 1999, p. 20.
5 Kevin Johnson, "Colo. Sheriff Is Feeling Strain, Friends Say," *USA Today*, May 10, 1999, p. 4A.
6 Daniel Glick, "Anatomy of a Massacre," *Newsweek*, May 3, 1999, p. 29.
7 "Gunmen's teacher had warned of violent writings," *New York Times*, May 11, 1999.
8 Glick, pp. 25-26.
9 Pooley, p. 29.
10 Notebook-Verbatim section, *Time*, May 3, 1999, p. 15.
11 Gibbs, p. 31.
12 Jodi Wilgoren and Dirk Johnson, "Sketch of 2 Killers: Contradictions and Confusion," *New York Times*, April 23, 1999.
13 Herbert.

14 Glick, p. 31.
15 Ibid.
16 Thomas Fields-Meyer, "United They Stand," *People*, May 10, 1999, pp. 68-73, and David Van Biema, "A Surge of Teen Spirit," *Time*, May 31, 1999, p. 59.
17 Charisse Jones, "Scars Might Never Fade for Victims, Their Families," *USA Today*, June 18, 1999, pp. 1A, 8A.
18 Ibid.
19 Tammerlin Drummond, "Battling the Columbine Copycats," [Online]. Available www.time.com, May 20, 1999.
20 Ibid.
21 Ibid.
22 Ibid.
23 Ibid.
24 " 'We're on Alert': Copycat Threats Disrupt Schools," *USA Today*, April 30, 1999.
25 Ibid.
26 Ibid.
27 Robert McFadden, "Violence, Real and Imagined, Sweeps Through Schools after the Shootings," *New York Times*, April 30, 1999.
28 "Michigan students charged in killing plot," *Minneapolis Star Tribune*, May 16, 1999.
29 Charisse Jones, "Deluge of Threats Paralyzing Schools," *USA Today*, May 19, 1999, p. 3A.
30 "Mich. Students Describe Plot for School Massacre," *USA Today*, May 28, 1999, p. 3A.
31 Cloud, p. 43.
32 Larry Copeland and Traci Watson, "Students Thought It Was a Prank," *USA Today*, May 21, 1999, p. 3A.
33 Joel Belz, "A Bull's-eye God," *World*, May 1, 1999, p. 7.
34 "Columbine High's Bittersweet Day," *Washington Post*, May 23, 1999.

Chapter 8—The Science (Fiction) of Teen Violence

1 Gibbs, p. 34.

2 CNN Interactive Quickvote: "Who or what is most responsible for school violence?" [Online]. Available http://cnn.com/POLL/results/128301.html.

3 [Online]. Available http://cgi.pathfinder.com/cig-bin/time/daily/gdml3/osform/generic.

4 Ann Oldenburg, " 'We're All Responsible' for Youth Violence," *USA Today,* May 11, 1999, p. 1D.

5 Erica Goode, "Deeper Truths Sought in Violence by Youths," *New York Times,* May 4, 1999.

6 H.J. Cummins, "Author Discusses Why Kids Turn Violent," *Minneapolis Star Tribune*, May 10, 1999, p. E2.

7 Kathy Kiely and Gary Fields, "Colo. Killers' Last Days Gave No Hint of Plans," *USA Today,* May 3, 1999.

8 Steisand and Cannon, p. 17.

9 Kiely and Fields.

10 Wilgoren and Johnson.

11 Gibbs, p. 34.

12 "3 Teens Detained During Massacre Cleared," *USA Today,* April 29, 1999.

13 Angie Cannon, "Kiss the Guns Goodbye?," *U.S. News & World Report*, May 31, 1999, p. 24.

14 Steisand and Cannon, p. 19.

15 Thomas L. Friedman, "Kosovo and Columbine," *New York Times*, May 4, 1999.

16 Sharon Begley, "Why the Young Kill," *Newsweek*, May 3, 1999, p. 32.

17 Ibid.

18 Anita Manning, "Chemistry of a Killer: Is It in Brain?," *USA Today*, April 29, 1999, p. 2A.

19 Leonard Pitts Jr., "Why? Maybe It's a Blessing Not to Know," *Chicago Tribune*, April 27, 1999, Section 1, p. 15.

20 Howard Chua-eoan, "Escaping from the Darkness," *Time*, May 31, 1999, p. 46.
21 Ibid.
22 Editorial, "What Is There to Say?," *Arkansas Democrat-Gazette*, March 21, 1998.
23 Stone Philips, *Weekend Magazine with Stone Philips*, MSNBC, May 2, 1999, 11 p.m. (EST).
24 Frank Pellegrini, "Littleton's Nobody's Fault—It's a Disease!" [Online]. Available http://cgi.pathfinder.com/time/daily/0,2960,24482, 00.html.

Part 2—Natural Born Causes

1 Rush Limbaugh, "The Rush Limbaugh Show," May 20, 1999.
2 Nancy Gibbs, "Noon in the Garden of Good and Evil," *Time*, May 17, 1999, p. 1.
3 Ibid., p. 25.
4 Jacquelyn Mitchard, "Not All Boys Who Wear Trenchcoats Are Bad Guys," *Minneapolis Star Tribune*, May 19, 1999.

Chapter 9—The Cause of Causes

1 Lloyd Cory, compiler, *Quote Unquote* (Wheaton, IL: Victor Press, 1977), p. 297.
2 C.S. Lewis, *Mere Christianity* (New York: Macmillan, 1960), p. 39.
3 Kristine Holmgren, "The Flaws of a Few Don't Make All of American Boyhood Evil," *Minneapolis Star Tribune*, May 14, 1999.
4 *20/20*, ABC-TV, May 21, 1999.
5 Jay Tolson, "The Vocabulary of Evil," *U.S. News & World Report*, May 10, 1999, p. 22.
6 Pooley, p. 32.
7 Tolson, p. 22.
8 Lloyd Cory, compiler, *Quote Unquote*, p. 297.

9 Pooley, p. 29.
10 Chua-eoan, "Six Friends Charged with Conspiracy," p. 54.
11 "Why Boys?," *Dateline*, NBC-TV, May 18, 1999.
12 Glick, p. 31.
13 Tolson, p. 22.

Chapter 10—Satanic Subversion

1 Ted and Virginia Byfield, "You Believe in God?," *Alberta Report*, May 17, 1999, p. 33.
2 EP News, April 30, 1999.
3 Charles E. Greenwalt II, "Media Profits Highly from Death Culture," *Harrisburg (PA) Patriot News*, May 9, 1999.
4 C.S. Lewis, *The Screwtape Letters* (New York: Macmillan, 1961), pp. 32-33.
5 Timothy M. Warner, *Spiritual Warfare* (Wheaton, IL: Crossway Books, 1991), p. 17.
6 Dennis Mullen, "Ambush at School" [Online]. Available http://members.aol.com/ billjr313/mhcc/sermon.html.
7 "Have We Grown Deaf to Plight of Alienated Teens?," *USA Today*, May 21, 1999, p. 14A.

Chapter 11—The Abortion Distortion

1 Mike Soraghan, "Letter's Abortion-Massacre Link 'Appalls' Senate after Tragedy," *Denver Post*, April 27, 1999, p. 8A.
2 Cal Thomas, "This Is Progress?," *World*, May 1, 1999, p. 18.
3 [Online]. Available http://www.duhaime.org/ca-abor.htm.
4 [Online]. Available http://www.solon.org/Constitutions/ Canada/English/ca-1982.html.
5 [Online]. Available http://www.duhaime.org/ca-abor.htm.
6 Ibid.
7 Ibid.
8 Dr. Frank Joseph, "The Site Where You Will Learn the Truth about the Killing of Unborn Babies" [Online]. Available http://members. aol.com/_ht_a/ dfjoseph/index.html.

9 Ibid.
10 "Killing a Baby Called Hope," *World,* May 1, 1999, p. 10.
11 Ibid.
12 Joseph [Online].
13 [Online]. Available http://www.controversygrrl.com/cgmassacre.html.
14 Chris Hawley, "Humane killing of whales considered" [Online]. Available www.ap.org, May 27, 1999.
15 Soraghan, p. 8A.
16 [Online]. Available http://www.controversygrrl.com/cgmassacre.html.
17 Taken from the Dr. Laura radio program, May 20, 1999; used by permission.
18 Jennifer Couzin, "The Promise and Peril of Stem Cell Research," *U.S. News & World Report,* May 31, 1999, p. 68.
19 Tim Friend, "OK to Fetal Tissue Research May Ignite Ethical Firestorm," *USA Today,* May 24, 1999, p. 1A.
20 Couzin, p. 68.
21 Friend, p. 2A.
22 Fanny J. Crosby, "Safe in the Arms of Jesus," from *Hymns of the Christian Life* (Camp Hill, PA: Christian Publications, 1978), p. 388.

Chapter 12—Parental Abdication

1 Ellen Goodman, "Before Punishing Parents for the Sins of Their Kids," *Boston Globe,* May 6, 1999.
2 Ibid.
3 William Glaberson, "What Did Parents Know, and Are They to Blame?," *New York Times,* April 27, 1999.
4 Ibid.
5 Ibid.
6 Goodman.
7 Glaberson.
8 Ibid.

9 April M. Washington, "Shoelses to Sue Parents of Harris, Klebold," *Denver Rocky Mountain News*, May 27, 1999, p. 5A.
10 "Family Sues Parents of Columbine Gunmen," *Minneapolis Star Tribune,* May 28, 1999, p. A4.
11 Ibid.
12 Ibid.
13 Susan Greene, "Mom Still Haunted by '97 Suicide," *Denver Post*, April 27, 1999, p. 1AA.
14 Ibid., p. 1AA, 8AA.
15 Ibid.
16 Goodman.
17 Ibid.
18 Syl Jones, "Instead of Teen Expose, Try Looking at 'The Secret Life of Adults,' " *Minneapolis Star Tribune,* May 7, 1999, p. A23.
19 Bill Owens, "Hold Parents Accountable," *USA Today,* April 29, 1999.
20 Amy Dickinson, "Where Were the Parents?," *Time*, May 3, 1999, p. 40.
21 Greenwalt.
22 Ibid.
23 Kim Ode, "We've Left It to Beaver," *Minneapolis Star Tribune,* p. E2.
24 Ibid.

Chapter 13—Virtual and Visual Violence

1 John Leo, "When Life Imitates Video," *U.S. News & World Report*, May 3, 1999, p. 14.
2 *Washington Watch,* July 1999, p. 1.
3 Chris Nashawaty, "The Hunger," *Entertainment Weekly,* May 7, 1999, p. 24.
4 Ibid.
5 Deirdre Donahue, "Frolicking in Gory Muck, This Tale of Lecter Is a Loser," *USA Today,* June 9, 1999, pp. 1D, 2D.

6 Nashawaty, p. 26.
7 Nancy Gibbs, "Special Report," *Time*, May 31, 1999, p. 33.
8 Steven Levy, "Loitering on the Dark Side," *Newsweek*, May 3, 1999, p. 39.
9 Greenwalt.
10 Bruce Haring, "Hairy Carrey rocks at MTV awards," *USA Today*, June 7, 1999, p. 3D.
11 Editorial, "The Gaming of Violence," *New York Times*, April 20, 1999.
12 Leo, p. 14.
13 David Grossman, "Trained to Kill," *Christianity Today*, August 10, 1998, p. 34.
14 Statistics quoted from lecture by Dr. James Garbarino, St. Paul, Minnesota, May 11, 1999, 3:30-5 p.m.
15 Grossman, "Trained to Kill," p. 37.
16 Leo, p. 14.
17 "The Gaming of Violence."
18 Interview with Dr. David Grossman, MSNBC, May 13, 1999, 10-11 a.m., EST.
19 Steve Alexander, "Author: Video Games Don't Cause Violence in Normal Teens," *Minneapolis Star Tribune*, May 14, 1999.
20 Joshua Quittner, "Are Video Games Really So Bad?," *Time*, May 10, 1999, p. 54.
21 Stephen Braun, "Do Shoot-'Em-Up Video Games Lead to Real-Life Youth Crimes?," *Los Angeles Times*, May 5, 1999.
22 Leo, p. 14.
23 Ibid.
24 Kevin Flynn, "Violent Video Games on DIA Departure List," *Denver Rocky Mountain News*, May 27, 1999.
25 "Scrutiny of Media Violence Has Experts Citing Studies," *New York Times*, May 9, 1999.
26 Ibid.
27 Ibid.

28 Ann Oldenburg and Mike Snider, "Entertainment in the Cross Hairs," *USA Today*, May 4, 1999, p. 1D.
29 Noel Holston, "As Violence Grows, Critics Debate Notion of Censorship," *Minneapolis Star Tribune*, May 9, 1999, p. F9.
30 Robert W. Butler, "Film Gore Once Shocking, Now Common," *Harrisburg (Pa.) Patriot-News*, May 4, 1999, p. D2.
31 Ibid.
32 Ibid.
33 Ibid.
34 Richard Corliss, "Bang, You're Dead," *Time*, May 3, 1999, p. 49.
35 Mike Snider, "Violent Entertainment Scrutinized," *USA Today*, May 5, 1999, p. 3A.
36 John Leo, "Gunning for Hollywood," *U.S. News & World Report*, May 10, 1999, p. 16.
37 Butler, p. D2.
38 Ibid.
39 Kristen Baldwin, "There's No Why," *Entertainment Weekly*, May 7, 1999, p. 9.
40 Maureen Dowd, "Washington's Matrix," *New York Times*, April 29, 1999.
41 Ibid.
42 Ibid.
43 "Violence Debate Convenes Today at White House" [Online]. Available www.ap.org, May 10, 1999.
44 "Clinton Calls Forum of Leaders in Effort to Stem Youth Violence," *New York Times*, May 1, 1999.
45 Joseph I. Lieberman and John McCain, "Toward a Safer Media Culture," *Minneapolis Star Tribune*, May 13, 1999, p. A19.
46 Steven Levy, "Loitering on the Dark Side," *Newsweek*, May 3, 1999, p. 39.
47 Ibid.
48 Ibid.
49 Ibid.

50 Ibid.
51 Thomas, p. 18.

Chapter 14—Musical Mayhem

1 Gene Edward Veith, "The Youth Anti-Culture," *World,* May 8, 1999, p. 25.
2 "Breaking All the Rules," recorded by Peter Frampton, quoted from *Hit Parader,* December, 1981, p. 46.
3 Tony Sanchez, *Up and Down with the Rolling Stones* (New York: New American Library, 1979), p. 127.
4 Jonathan Green, compiler, *The Book of Rock Quotes* (New York: Omnibus Press, 1977), p. 54.
5 Ibid., p. 67.
6 Bob Larson, *The Day Music Died* (Carol Stream, IL: Creation House, 1972), pp. 53-54.
7 "Death at the Coliseum: The Night That Shook the World of Rock," *Families,* Vol. 1 (October, 1981), p. 108.
8 "How the Entertained Are Warned," *USA Today,* May 4, 1999, p. 6D.
9 Veith, p. 25.
10 Ibid.
11 Ibid.
12 Ibid.
13 "Welcome to the World of KMFDM" [Online]. Available http://www. KMFDM.com.
14 Ibid.
15 Ibid.
16 Ibid.
17 Ibid.
18 Ibid.
19 Ann Powers, "The Stresses of Youth, the Strains of Its Music," *New York Times,* April 25, 1999.
20 Ibid.

21 "Shock-Rocker Cuts Tour Short Because of School Massacre," *Minneapolis Star Tribune*, April 29, 1999.
22 "The Marilyn Manson Charnel" [Online]. Available http://www. marilyn-manson.net.
23 Ibid.
24 Ibid.
25 Marilyn Manson, "Columbine: Whose Fault Is It?" [Online]. Available http://www. rollingstone.com.
26 Ibid.
27 Susan Hogan/Albach, "Massacre at Alma Mater Shocks Singer Erik Sundin," *Minneapolis Star Tribune*, May 1, 1999.

Chapter 15—http://www.pipebomb.com

1 Friedman.
2 Wilgoren and Johnson.
3 Ibid.
4 Steven Levy, "Loitering on the Dark Side," *Newsweek*, May 3, 1999, p. 39.
5 Thomas L. Friedman, "Judgment Not Included," *New York Times*, April 27, 1999.
6 Amy Harmon, "Parents Fear That Children Are One Click Ahead," *New York Times*, May 3, 1999.
7 Ibid.
8 Industry Standard staff, "Why and how much kids go online" [Online]. Available http://cnn.com/TECH/computing/9808/11/kidsonline.idg/index.html.
9 CNN Interactive, "Poll: Parents aren't watching 'Net-surfing teens" [Online]. Available http://cnn.com/ US/9905/01/teen.poll/index.html.
10 Friedman, "Judgment Not Included."
11 Ibid.
12 Ibid.

Chapter 16—The Wrong of Rights

1 Wayne R. LaPierre, reporting to the U.S. House Judiciary Committee's Subcommittee on Crime, taken from *USA Today,* June 1, 1999, p. 19A.

2 Taken from *Compton's Interactive Encyclopedia,* Version 2.01VW, 1994.

3 "Quotables," *World,* May 8, 1999, p. 12.

4 Peter Johnson, "Free-Speech Forces Don't Defend Jones," *USA Today,* May 10, 1999, p. 3D.

5 Ibid.

6 Ibid.

7 Ibid.

8 KXPK-FM, Denver, Colorado, April 21, 1999.

9 Mike Snider, "Violent Entertainment Scrutinized," *USA Today,* May 5, 1999, p. 3A.

10 Joshua Quittner, "Are Video Games Really So Bad?," *Time*, May 10, 1999, p. 54.

11 Snider, p. 3A.

12 Leo, "Gunning for Hollywood," p. 16.

13 "More Gun Laws Won't Help, NRA Figure Says," *Minneapolis Star Tribune,* May 23, 1999, p. A13.

14 "Kids Find Guns Easy to Get, Study Says," *Lancaster (Pa.) Sunday News,* May 23, 1999, p. A-15.

15 Ibid.

16 Bob von Sternburg, "In Canada, Fewer Guns and Less Violence," *Minneapolis Star Tribune*, May 16, 1999, p. A7.

17 Ibid.

18 Ibid.

19 Ibid.

20 Ibid.

21 Ibid.

22 Ibid.

23 Margaret Carlson, "An Outrage That Will Last," *Time*, May 10, 1999, p. 35.

24 Leo, "Gunning for Hollywood," p. 16, quoting critic Mark Crispin Miller.

Part 3—The Supernatural Cure

1 Cummins, p. E2, quoting Dr. James Garbarino.
2 Claudia Puig, "Hollywood Examines Its Soul," *USA Today,* June 7, 1999, p. 1D.

Chapter 17—The Victor over Violence

1 William R. Newell, "At Calvary," *Hymns of the Christian Life* (Camp Hill, PA: Christian Publications, 1978), p. 479.
2 Crosson.
3 James Kullander, "God, on Our Own Terms," *New York Times,* October 26, 1998.

Chapter 18—Satan's Defeat: Then, Now and Forever

1 A.W. Tozer, *I Talk Back to the Devil* (Camp Hill, PA: Christian Publications, 1972), p. 21.
2 Dan Mayhew [Online]. Available e-mail: summit@worldaccessnet.com, May 21, 1999.
3 Edward Plowman, "Faith at Gunpoint," *World,* May 8, 1999, p. 14.
4 Warner, p. 56.

Chapter 19—Revival from a Rampage

1 Gibbs, "Noon in the Garden of Good and Evil."
2 Deborah Sharp, "17-year-old's Last Words Inspire Other Christians," *USA Today,* June 1, 1999, p. 3A.
3 Eileen McNamara, "Student Affirmed Her Belief in God, and Then Was Slain," *Boston Globe*, April 24, 1999, p. A01.

4 Van Biema, p. 58.
5 Byfield, p. 33.
6 Charles W. Colson, "Littleton's Martyrs," *Washington Post*, April 26, 1999.
7 Ibid.
8 Bill Scanlon, " 'She Said Yes' to Tell Cassie Bernall's Story," *Denver Rocky Mountain News*, June 4, 1999.
9 Janet Bingham, "Cassie Died a Martyr's Death," *Denver Post*, April 27, 1999.
10 Ibid.
11 Gibbs, "Noon in the Garden of Good and Evil."
12 Sharp, p. 3A.
13 Byfield, p. 33.
14 Van Biema, p. 59.
15 Plowman, p. 17.
16 Ibid.
17 *Washington Watch*, July 1999, p. 1.
18 Ibid., p. 4.
19 Ibid.
20 Plowman, p. 17.

Epilogue—The Final Solution

1 A.W. Tozer, *The Knowledge of the Holy* (New York: Harper and Row, 1975), p. 62.

Special Offer

If you made a first-time commitment to become a Christian as a result of reading this book, I would like to send you something to help you live a Christian life and grow in the Christian faith. Please fill out the form below, add a brief personal testimony and mail it to:

Tom Allen's Special Offer
Christian Publications
3825 Hartzdale Drive
Camp Hill, PA 17011

YES! I prayed to receive Christ as my Savior as a result of reading Tom Allen's book, *With No Remorse*. Please send me the free special offer. I have included a brief testimony of my decision.

NAME:

____

ADDRESS:

____

CITY:

____

STATE/PROVINCE:

____

ZIP/POSTAL CODE:

____

Other books by Tom Allen:

10 Stupid Things Christians Do to Stunt Their Growth

A Closer Look at Dr. Laura

Joy Comes in the Mourning (with Dave Johnson)

Booklets by Tom Allen:

Spiritual Leadership Begins at Home

Let Him That Is without Sin . . .

Hope for Hurting Parents